THE INNOCENCE OF SEDUCTION

The Innocence Of Seduction

ISBN-13: 978-1957328355

Cover art by Tony Donley

For information about production rights, contact:
mark.pracht@gmail.com

Published by Sordelet Ink

THE INNOCENCE OF SEDUCTION

A PLAY BY
MARK PRACHT

PART TWO OF THE FOUR-COLOR TRILOGY

SORDELET
ink

DEDICATION

For Colene.

If only I could take it all upon myself.

THE INNOCENCE OF SEDUCTION was originally produced at City Lit Theatre in Chicago, IL from Aug 25th to Oct 8th, 2023. Directed by Mark Pracht, Stage management by Zachary Osterman, Scenic, Lighting and Projection Design by G. "Max" Maxim IV, Costume Design by Beth Laske-Miller, Original Music composed by Petter Wahlback, Violence and Intimacy Design by Alison Dornheggen, and Original Artwork created by Tony Donley.

The original cast was as follows:

WILLIAM "BILL" GAINES — SEAN HARKLERODE

AL FELDSTEIN — CHARLIE DIAZ

DOCTOR FREDERIC WERTHAM — FRANK NALL

MATT BAKER — BRAIN BRADFORD

JANICE VALLEAU — MEGAN CLARKE

LYLE STUART — ZACH KUNDE

SHIRLEY NORRIS — LAURA COLEMAN

MAX GAINE — RON QUADE

ARCHER ST JOHN

HENRY VALLEAU — JOHN BLICK

JUDGE CHARLES F MURPHY

BARRY WALSH — CHUCK MUNRO

JOHN L GOLDWATER/SENATOR HENDRICKSON — PAUL CHAKRIN

CONNIE/SECRETARY — LATORIOUS R GIVENS

EVERETT M "BUSY" ARNOLD/SENATOR KEFAUVER — ROBIN TREVINO

FRANK GUISTO/JACK DAVIS/REED CRANDALL — ANDREW BOSWORTH

JESSIE GAINES/GERTRUDE ST JOHN — JESSICA LAUREN FISHER

"Comics are one of the five native American art forms, including banjo music, jazz music, musical theatre, and the mystery story as invented by Edgar Allen Poe."

— *Harlan Ellison*

"Being like everybody is the same as being nobody."

— *Rod Serling*

Cast of Characters

WILLIAM "BILL" GAINES
AL FELDSTEIN
DOCTOR FREDERIC WERTHAM
MATT BAKER
JANICE VALLEAU
LYLE STUART
SHIRLEY NORRIS
ARCHER ST JOHN
EVERETT M "BUSY" ARNOLD
FRANK GUISTO
MAX GAINES
CONNIE
REED CRANDALL
JOHN L GOLDWATER
JUDGE CHARLES F MURPHY
SENATOR ESTES KEFAUVER
SENATOR ROBERT C HENDRICKSON
JESSIE GAINES
JACK DAVIS
GERTRUDE ST JOHN
HENRY VALLEAU
BARRY WALSH
SECRETARY (VOICE ONLY)

FOREWORD

The play you are holding was part of my great "COVID project." A time when I was truly fearful that I would ever see a theatre full of an enraptured audience ever again. What has also happened since our great pause is that I also find myself fearful about the ability of artists to freely pursue their creative impulses. We again find comics and graphic storytelling at the center of controversy. From Maia Kobabe's GENDER QUEER to Art Spiegelman's MAUS. We find, much like with the Comics Code Authority, forces from within our own creative communities acting to limit the work of their peers.

I'm a firm believer in art and creativity, and I think that storytelling and imagination can open doors. That process is always fraught. Artists open their hearts and bring not only the best of themselves, but also the worst. That is the honesty that can foster understanding and build bridges. As my version of Matt Baker says in the following pages, "put your heart into your work, and you'll offend somebody."

The legacy of EC Comics is that of blindingly progressive (for the time) social commentary, satire and critique. It is also that of sophomoric humor, shocking transgression and bad taste. It is all of those things that made the work pioneered by Bill Gaines, Al Feldstein, and the "usual gang of idiots" so vital and, with the lens of history, important.

As time went on, the astoundingly positive response and support I've received from the productions of the first two plays (with part three set for the Fall of 2024), leads me to believe that the performing arts can and will survive. Even saying that, we need to give people a compelling reason to spend a few hours with our work. It's our job to communicate, to engage and entertain.

My main goal is always to entertain. If a bit of enlightenment about a time when this very uniquely American art form flirted with extinction can mix with a bit of laughter and pathos? I can feel that I've achieved all I could hope. If you're laughing, you're seeing the humanity that connects us all.

As to the play you've purchased (thank you!), as always, I must note, THE INNOCENCE OF SEDUCTION is a fiction. Details, characters and timelines have been adjusted for dramatic effect. I encourage you, if you are compelled by Bill, Matt, and Janice's story, to seek out the books, websites and documentaries that tell the full story.

NOTES

This story is loosely based on actual events and people. In certain case incidents, characters and timelines have been changed for dramatic purposes. Certain characters may be composites, or entirely fictitious.

"EC Comics," "Tales From The Crypt" and associated titles are copyright and trademark of William M. Gaines Agent, Inc. They are used in a narrative, historical context, and no ownership is implied.

"MAD Magazine" is copyright and trademark of Warner Brothers Publications, and used in a narrative, historical context. No ownership is implied.

A note on projections: These should be dynamic, brief, and not intrude into the scenes. Dialogue should be continuous.

THE INNOCENCE OF SEDUCTION

ACT I

Scene One

(The lights rise. A desk, littered with various crime and horror comics of the 1950's. Behind it, a bespectacled, gaunt, cadaverous, ghoulish figure that invokes thoughts of the EC Comics Crypt-Keeper. This is DOCTOR FREDRIC WERTHAM, and he speaks to us with a deep German accent...)

WERTHAM
Hello, there my sweet little *schöne kinder*, how lovely you all look today! My name is Doctor Fredric Wertham. I have practiced psychiatry and neurology since 1922. Some part of my research in that time was on paresis and brain syphilis.

How very horrible that was...The stuff of nightmares. One poor man could not stop screaming...

It came in good stead when I came to study comic books! Some of these comic books are before me here. Such as this one, in particular.

(He waves a comic book, quickly, so as the title and issue

are completely missed)

(Projected: CITATION MISSING)

WERTHAM

Here is the lecherous-looking bandit overpowering the attractive girl, who is dressed...If that is the word for it... For very hot weather. "She could come in handy, then!" He bellows, "pretty little spitfire, eh!"...In the typical pre-rape position. Here is the repetition of violence and sexiness which no Freud, Krafft-Ebing or Havelock Ellis ever dreamed could be offered to children, and in such profusion.

(Projected: an image of teen "delinquents" of the 1950's)

WERTHAM

I examined a boy who had threatened a woman teacher with a switchblade knife. He was enthusiastic about comic books filled with alluring tales of shooting, knifing, hitting and strangling. Everywhere children see this, and finally they become, as Saint Augustine said...Unconsciously delighted. Innocents seduced by the bestial nightmare of a moral apocalypse foisted by a corrupt industry.

(Lights shift)

Scene Two

(Lights shift to a darkened office, WILLIAM "BILL" GAINES appears behind the office desk, sleeping, face down on the blotter)

WERTHAM
Here, we find the beast himself. A pathetic man-child with deep, psychological scars.

(WERTHAM recedes into the shadows. The voice of MAX, GAINES' father, floats out of the darkness)

MAX
William!!

(GAINES shifts, but does not awake)

MAX
Why must you always disappoint me!?!

(MAX steps into the light, looming over his son's sleeping form. He is dripping with water, his face and chest torn with gore and gristle. He grabs the younger man, GAINES awakes, sees the gruesome form of his father, and screams)

MAX
LOOK AT ME!! YOU DID THIS TO ME!! It's your fault! You broke your mother's heart. She spent months to convince Hazel that you were worth her time. All you had to do was be a good husband, and you failed!!

(MAX begins to remove his belt)

GAINES
I tried!!

MAX
IT WASN'T GOOD ENOUGH!!

(MAX raises his belt above his head, about to strike)

MAX
YOU'RE NEVER GOOD ENOUGH!!

(GAINES Screams, and falls behind his desk, the specter of his father swings the leather strap downward. Blackout. Another voice, of SHIRLEY NORRIS, his secretary, comes from the darkness)

SHIRLEY
Mister Gaines?

GAINES
DEAR GOD, NO!! HELP ME!!!!

(The lights come on in Gaines' office, he is still crying out, hidden behind the desk. Shirley is standing in the doorway)

SHIRLEY
Mister Gaines!? Are you all right!?

(Long beat)

GAINES
Yes?

SHIRLEY
I heard something.

GAINES
What? Oh, nothing. Just my new hi-fi system.

SHIRLEY
It sounded like screaming.

GAINES
Oh, that! It's one of those spook-house sound effects records. "The Chilling Sounds of Terror."

SHIRLEY
Why are you on the floor?

GAINES
Back problems! Trying to relax it. Nothing to worry about.

SHIRLEY
Your mother is here.

GAINES
Oh dear God.

(GAINES' head slowly rises into view from behind the desk)

GAINES
Tell her I'm out?

SHIRLEY
I think she heard you screaming.

(He sinks back behind the desk. Beat)

SHIRLEY
I'll just bring her in then?

(The secretary turns and begins to exit)

SHIRLEY
That is a weird guy.

(*SHIRLEY exits, GAINES rises. He straightens his shirt and makes a half-hearted attempt to compose himself. He picks up a photo from the desk*)

(*Projected: A photo of a non-undead Max Gaines*)

GAINES
Bastard.

(*JESSIE GAINES enters the room in a whirlwind*)

JESSIE
My God, William, what were you doing in here?

GAINES
Hello, mother.

JESSIE
You haven't been home.

GAINES
Well, you forced me into running a company. It takes up a lot of my time.

(*JESSIE runs a finger over the edge of the desk, checks the tip for dust*)

JESSIE
Shirley out there tells me you spend most of your time sleeping.

GAINES
Well...I don't think that's any of her business.

JESSIE
It isn't, it's MY business. Your father built Educational Comics from the ground up, nothing else was important to him.

GAINES
I'll try not to take that personally.

JESSIE
Oh don't whine, William.

GAINES
It's Entertaining Comics now.

(Beat)

JESSIE
Your father is probably rolling in his grave.

(GAINES looks about nervously, expecting MAX to appear)

GAINES
Probably.

JESSIE
How could you do this to him?

GAINES
Mother, Dad was losing money! What do you expect ME to do?

JESSIE
That can't be true.

GAINES
No one wants to read Picture Stories From The Bible! No kids, no adults, no one! I think we have to assume that you can't be successful if the only people buying your product are nuns and Sunday school teachers!

JESSIE
An affront to your father's legacy.

GAINES
I don't want this job. I never did, you forced it on me.

JESSIE
If only you'd been able to keep Hazel happy.

GAINES
If only you hadn't forced me to marry my second cousin.

(JESSIE slaps him)

JESSIE
I did what you couldn't, or wouldn't, do for yourself. Hazel was a lovely girl, and you failed her. Now you're going to fail your father!

GAINES
(Quietly) All I wanted was to teach chemistry.

JESSIE
I wanted to grow old with your father, but an out-of-control speedboat tore him to shreds.

GAINES
Always with the speedboat.

JESSIE
You have a duty to me, his memory, and the family name.

(JESSE marches out of the room. GAINES sits silently behind his desk for a moment)

GAINES
I wonder if I could pay that speedboat to run me over?

(Lights shift)

Scene Three

(WERTHAM steps back out of the dark)

WERTHAM
Mein Gott, Mister Gaines is a damaged personality! Arrested in his development, bordering on retardation, and prone to fantasies of violence and persecution. Unfortunately, as you will see, he longs to share this condition like a psychological plague through his grotesque "art" and unseemly "publications."

(Projected: A series of pre-code panels featuring violence and sexual content)

WERTHAM
Of course, he was not alone. An entire industry rose up to claw at the ripe young mind of the American child!!

(Lights shift, and WERTHAM slips back into the darkness. Lights up on the office of JOHN L GOLDWATER, publisher of MLJ Comics. He sits behind his desk, shuffling papers. The door opens, and JANICE VALLEAU sticks her head in the door)

JANICE
Mister Goldwater? You asked to see me?

GOLDWATER
Janice! My secretary tells me I won't be seeing your smiling face after today. I am not happy about this. I'm going to be stuck looking at that pack of sad-sack mugs out there every morning.

JANICE
If you paid them better, they wouldn't be such sad-sacks.

GOLDWATER
Y'know, it wasn't that long ago that the idea of a woman working in this business was unthinkable. That's what happens when you have a boom. Anybody who walks in the door that can draw more than a stick figure gets hired.

JANICE
Is that what you think of my work?

GOLDWATER
Hardly! I kept waiting for you to get tired of the Betty and Veronica backups, and try to knock that dunderhead Bob Montana out of a job on the main feature.

JANICE
Bob is VERY CLOSE to reading now. Way past dunder-headed.

GOLDWATER
(Laughs) Always the go-getter. I'm honestly surprised you aren't moving into my office.

JANICE
I needed to knock Bob off, first. I tried everything, poison, knives, booby traps...

GOLDWATER
Just shoot him. If it's worth doing, it's worth overdoing.

JANICE
Noted.

GOLDWATER
Quality's not going to pay you any more than I am.

JANICE
I don't think that's any of your business, Mister Goldwater.

GOLDWATER
Janice, I have lunch with Busy Arnold twice a week.

JANICE
That so?

GOLDWATER
You want to work with Reed Crandall.

JANICE
He IS the best, Mister Goldwater.

GOLDWATER
Janice, in 24 hours you won't be my employee anymore. In that spirit? I'm going to give you some advice. Don't get star-struck.

JANICE
I'm not star-struck.

GOLDWATER
This business is no damn good.

JANICE
How can you say that?

GOLDWATER
Oh, it's made me a good living. I'm not discounting that.

JANICE
Then what?

GOLDWATER
We peddle trash, Janice. *(He holds up an issue of Archie comics)* Archie and Jughead are basically luke-warm water, and that's what keeps me above the slime. There are people watching us, and they don't like what they see.

JANICE
But I do.

GOLDWATER
Young lady, that's just crazy talk.

JANICE
It's my crazy talk.

GOLDWATER
OK, just trying to give you some advice.

JANICE
I can take care of myself.

GOLDWATER
Clearly. I just want you to remember what I said. Every boom ends. The job isn't drawing the pages. The job is finding the next job. Everyone is expendable. One month of bad sales away from being on the street.

(GOLDWATER shakes her hand)

GOLDWATER
Miss Janice Valleau, MLJ comics will, officially, miss you. Good luck over at Quality.

JANICE
Maybe I'll drop by from time to time to remind you all of what you're missing.

GOLDWATER
Don't take any guff from Busy Arnold.

(JANICE rises to leave)

GOLDWATER
Usually when one of my artists quits, I just sign a final check and shove them out the door. What is this power you hold over grumpy old men?

JANICE
I'm a younger woman.

(She opens the office door)

JANICE
Onward and upward!

(JANICE exits. Lights shift)

SCENE FOUR

(WERTHAM steps out of the darkness)

WERTHAM
Such a pretty little fräulein, Miss Valleau. You may look at her and see an innocent young girl. A fabrication! An insidious vixen using her budding sexuality to manipulate these poor, innocent men.

(Projected: a series of Matt Baker cheesecake images from various books)

WERTHAM
Comic books stimulate children sexually. A twelve-year-old sex delinquent told me "In comic books sometimes the men threaten the girls. They don't get me sexually excited all the time, only when they tie them up."

(The lights shift and we see MATT BAKER in a room with ARCHER ST JOHN and his friend, FRANK GUISTO. They are poring over art boards)

ST JOHN
Do you think it's too sexy? Sex sells, but...

BAKER
I'm not drawing for kids here, but I'm not pushing pornography on you, Archer.

(ST JOHN *holds up the art board to the other two men*)

(Projected: *The cover of* IT RHYMES WITH LUST)

ST JOHN
No one ever called me a prude, but, I mean, c'mon. Wertham will have a field day with some of this.

BAKER
That twisted old quack sees what he wants to see.

(ST JOHN *pulls a bottle from an office bar and pours a generous glass*)

ST JOHN
You've got a book here that's sex or violence on virtually every page.

BAKER
I didn't say it was Pollyanna. It's supposed to reach a wider...an older, audience. It's not really a comic book.

ST JOHN
You could fool me, Matt. Panels, word balloons.

GUISTO
It's a whole new thing. A picture novel, long form comic storytelling.

BAKER
Frank...

ST JOHN
Matt, who is this guy?

BAKER
Frank Guisto.

GUISTO
Colleague and Best friend!

ST JOHN
You don't say...

GUISTO
Known each other for years.

ST JOHN
And you bring him to a business meeting?

BAKER
He's...

GUISTO
It's a more developed comic book. A deliberate bridge between comic books and "book" books.

ST JOHN
Are you his friend, or his agent?

(Beat)

GUISTO
Little of both?

BAKER
This could be a new thing. A series of action, mystery, western and romance movies...on paper.

(ST JOHN has finished his drink and pours another)

ST JOHN
I've heard the pitch two or three times, between you and the writer. Four if you count this squirrelly kid, here. Drink?

GUISTO
I'd sure...

BAKER
We're good. The idea is to redefine the business. Open it up to adults, as well as kids.

ST JOHN
Reads like a soap opera.

BAKER
Black and white, a paperback. Not stocked with the comic books, or even the magazines.

ST JOHN
That might get Wertham off our backs.

BAKER
Wertham will blow over. This could open a whole new audience.

ST JOHN
Blow over? Have you heard him?

BAKER
Who listens to that kind of nonsense?

ST JOHN
You'd be surprised.

(ST JOHN holds up a page to BAKER)

(Projected: an image of Rust Masson from IT RHYMES WITH LUST)

ST JOHN
Rust Masson doesn't exactly look like a nun, but I guess that is why we hired you, Matt.

GUISTO
I'm an artist, too. I thought maybe I could pitch a couple ideas of my own...

ST JOHN
No.

GUISTO
Hey, c'mon! I may not sling the cheesecake like Matt, but I got the goods!

ST JOHN
One stud is all we need, around here.

BAKER
What does that mean?

ST JOHN
I just hear tell you're a, uh, ladies man.

BAKER
My private life, and how I spend it, is none of your business.

(Beat)

ST JOHN
I respect that.

BAKER
I sincerely hope so.

ST JOHN
You might be surprised how much.

(Beat)

BAKER
Mister St John...

ST JOHN
Please call me Archer.

BAKER
Look, Mister St John, I think we've got a book that people will like...

ST JOHN
Let's get more social. I know a place...

GUISTO
Sounds great!

(Beat. ST JOHN side-eyes GUISTO)

ST JOHN
Let me clarify. MATT, since my office liquor isn't tempting, would YOU like to get a drink someplace more casual? I was thinking we could drop by Stewart's.

BAKER
Stewart's Cafeteria?

ST JOHN
Yeah. You know the place?

BAKER
I've...heard of it.

ST JOHN
Well, they know me there. You'd be welcome. Let me get my coat.

(ST JOHN steps out)

GUISTO
Well, nobody ever said Frank Guisto doesn't know a cue when he hears it.

BAKER
Frank, don't...

GUISTO
Matt. I try to be a worldly, open-minded man, but I know when I need to bow out.

(GUISTO exits. ST JOHN re-enters)

ST JOHN
Ready to go?

BAKER
What are you after, Mister Saint John?

ST JOHN
Matt. Call me Archer. It'll be fun. I promise you'll be right at home.

(ST JOHN reaches out and places his palm lightly on BAKER's chest. Lights shift)

Scene Five

(WERTHAM steps out of the darkness)

WERTHAM
Well, well, well....Isn't THAT interesting? I wouldn't dare assume anything, of course, being a man of science, but...They seem to be heading for a gay old time, as they say. *(Chuckles)* The time when children are most susceptible to social and psychological influences is in their leisure hours. Have no doubt, children's leisure is on the market. Of course children also get hurt at home and by their parents.

(The lights shift to a shadowy GAINES' office at EC Comics. GAINES is face-down on his desk. A large profit graph is projected, with a downward trajectory. The Undead MAX emerges from the shadows)

MAX
Well, now you've done it. You killed me, and then you killed my company.

SHIRLEY *(off stage)*
Mister Gaines?

MAX
It was my legacy!

SHIRLEY *(off stage)*
MISTER GAINES!!

(Lights full up. SHIRLEY stands before GAINES. His head rises from the desk. MAX freezes)

SHIRLEY
YOUR THREE O'CLOCK IS HERE!!

(Beat)

SHIRLEY
Should I show him in?

(GAINES stares at her, then at the specter of his father)

GAINES
I guess?

(SHIRLEY sighs, then turns to leave)

SHIRLEY
Mother told me working here was a one-way ticket to the funny farm.

(She exits. MAX springs back to life)

MAX
You failed me, William!

(Lights back up and MAX vanishes. AL FELDSTEIN has entered, unnoticed by GAINES)

GAINES
(To MAX) WELL AT LEAST I'M NOT AN ASSHOLE!!!

FELDSTEIN
I'll let you know after the meeting.

GAINES
How did you get in here?

FELDSTEIN
Your secretary let me in.

(Beat)

FELDSTEIN
We had a three o'clock?

GAINES
We did?

FELDSTEIN
Yeah. I'm Al Feldstein.

(He extends his hand, which GAINES seems to not notice)

GAINES
Right, OK…The artist with the "headlight" girls?

FELDSTEIN
What can I say? I like boobs.

(GAINES takes the portfolio, places it on his desk. He opens the portfolio, removes his glasses, places them carefully in a case, and drops his face inches above the paper. His nose is nearly resting upon it)

(Examples of FELDSTEIN's "headlight girls" from "Junior" comics are projected)

(GAINES flips several pages, repeating his close observation like a dippy-bird. His head shakes as he chuckles)

GAINES
You weren't kidding! Headlight girls? Hooo Boy! More like kleig lights!

FELDSTEIN
Well, I…

GAINES
They're bigger than her head!

(GAINES' face rises from the sample, he looks at FELDSTEIN)

GAINES
Do you use live models?

(There is uncomfortable moment of silence. Then GAINES barks a laugh)

FELDSTEIN
Was that a joke?

GAINES
What was your name again?

FELDSTEIN
Feldstein. Al.

GAINES
Well, you can draw.

FELDSTEIN
I write too. I usually get saddled with romance books...

GAINES
What? You don't want to do "Picture Stories From the Bible?"

FELDSTEIN
I would think a Virgin Mary with a double D cup would be frowned upon.

GAINES
Depends who's reading it.

FELDSTEIN
When was the last time you published one of those Bible comics? Has to be back before your father died.

(Lights darken as if MAX will reappear. GAINES reacts. FELDSTEIN does not. The lights shift back)

GAINES
Don't say that too loud!

FELDSTEIN
Why?

(GAINES leans forward. Waves to FELDSTEIN to lean in. Looks around)

GAINES
(Whispers) The walls. Have ears.

(Beat)

FELDSTEIN
OK.

GAINES
Did your father love you?

FELDSTEIN
Excuse me?

GAINES
My father hated me. This company meant more to him.

FELDSTEIN
At least he didn't ignore you.

GAINES
I'd have preferred that.

FELDSTEIN
No, you wouldn't.

(Beat)

FELDSTEIN
He was an artist, then he wasn't. He didn't give a damn about the excitements of his son.

GAINES
I wanted to teach chemistry, and somehow I ended up publishing comics.

FELDSTEIN
Mister Gaines, What makes you happy?

GAINES
Teaching chemistry.

FELDSTEIN
How long did you do that?

GAINES
I never did.

FELDSTEIN
Then how do you know it would make you happy?

(Beat)

GAINES
I want to get out front with something. They do a romance book, we do a romance book, they do a crime book, we do a crime book. Always playing catch up.

FELDSTEIN
Something new? How about Pyschoanalysis?

GAINES
What about it!?

FELDSTEIN
I was just trying to think of something ridiculous.

GAINES
Psychoanalysis is NOT ridiculous.

FELDSTEIN
Of course not, but it'd be a pretty silly comic book.

GAINES
It's not silly.

FELDSTEIN
(Chuckles) What, are you in therapy?

(Lights shift, WERTHAM appears)

WERTHAM
Hmmm...You thought I made it all up didn't you?

(The lights shift, WERTHAM disappears)

GAINES
That doesn't matter! I just want something that's OURS, something no one else has done...

FELDSTEIN
Like what? Something shocking? That's pretty tough, with all those crime books. They're doing no holds barred stuff.

GAINES
Well, gee, Al...You want a job? What would YOU do?

(FELDSTEIN considers for a moment)

FELDSTEIN
Do you remember that old radio show Inner Sanctum?

GAINES
Oh sure! I loved it! Creepy as all hell. Scared the shit out of me.

FELDSTEIN
Well, what if...we did that?

GAINES
Horror?

FELDSTEIN
Monsters, psycho killers, vampires, the whole nine yards. I mean, if the kids go crazy for murderous drug fiends and gangsters, why not give them rotting corpses?

GAINES
Rotting Corpses?

(Lights shift. MAX's arm comes from behind GAINES' chair and grabs him. GAINES yelps in fear. FELDSTEIN is oblivious)

FELDSTEIN
Are you OK, Mr. Gaines?

GAINES
Yeah, yeah...just...someone walked over my grave.

FELDSTEIN
(Laughs) Well, that's exactly the idea.

(GAINES gets up and looks behind his chair, and about the room)

FELDSTEIN
Mister Gaines?

(FELDSTEIN continues to look around the room)

FELDSTEIN
Should I come back later?

(GAINES looks behind one more set piece)

GAINES
He's gone.

FELDSTEIN
Who?

GAINES
I'm not crazy.

FELDSTEIN
I didn't think you were...Maybe the best thing to publish is what YOU want to read.

(Beat)

GAINES
You like Ray Bradbury?

FELDSTEIN
Love him.

GAINES
Lovecraft? Poe?

FELDSTEIN
Who doesn't?

GAINES
Can you do this with me? Run this book?

FELDSTEIN
Are you hiring me?

GAINES
Of course, of course! What the hell do you think we're talking about here? One story every day. I'll bring in three or four ideas, and we'll pitch stories to each other. You take your favorite and write it up.

FELDSTEIN
What are we gonna call it?

GAINES
"The Crypt of Terror?"

FELDSTEIN
Hmmm…that's OK, but what about "Tales From the Crypt?"

GAINES
Six of one, half dozen of the other.

FELDSTEIN
Maybe some sort of host, like those old radio shows?

GAINES
Whatever, you figure it out.

(FELDSTEIN offers his hand. GAINES stares at it)

GAINES
It's a whole new trend, Al.

(GAINES removes his glasses and begins perusing FELDSTEIN's art again. Awkward moment. FELDSTEIN, realizing he's been dismissed, makes his way out, passing SHIRLEY)

SHIRLEY
Mister Gaines? Your mother...

GAINES
You know what you can tell her, Shirley!?

SHIRLEY
Oh, please. Wow me.

(Beat)

GAINES
(Bravado gone) I'll talk to her when I get home.

SHIRLEY
I thought so.

(SHIRLEY turns to exit)

GAINES
...and send her some flowers. Maybe?

SHIRLEY
This family...I need a shower.

(SHIRLEY exits, GAINES is alone. The lights shift, MAX howls. GAINES screams and dives back behind his desk)

SCENE SIX

(Once again, WERTHAM steps out of the darkness)

WERTHAM

I can hear some of you...what can be the harm, Herr Doctor Wertham? They're only comic books! This reminds one of the old story of the boy called into conference by his father to receive sexual enlightenment. After a tedious discourse about the flowers, the birds and the bees, the boy interrupts his father impatiently, "there is no intercourse at all?" So one might ask about comic books: nobody gets shot? Or stabbed or tortured? No girls beaten, choked or almost raped? All this that the present-day child is exposed to. Vomited from the sickened minds of the depraved young men who dream up this filth...

(Lights shift. The offices of Quality Comics, JANICE VALLEAU is hunched over a drawing table, REED CRANDALL is stationed at a desk nearby. As the lights come up, Janice has spilled her ink on the page she has been working on)

JANICE
GODDAMMIT, MOTHERFUCKER!!

CRANDALL
Woah, woah!! Busy hired you to class up the joint.

JANICE
Reed, I spilled ink all over your page! This is just a disaster. How am I gonna clean this up? I've ruined it!

(CRANDALL looks at the page)

CRANDALL
Give me an hour, I'll re-draw it.

JANICE
You can't do that. I screwed it up.

CRANDALL
Ahh, Sure I can. Janice. It happens. Forget about it.

JANICE
I finally get to work on something great, and I botch it right away

CRANDALL
"Great?" You need your eyes checked. Plus, don't sell yourself short. That Archie stuff you did was fun.

JANICE
You'd never do it, Reed.

CRANDALL
THAT. Is incorrect. Also, I couldn't do it.

JANICE
Lies.

CRANDALL
I was never good with the cartoony stuff. You're a hell of an artist, Janice, the Toni Gayle stuff was great.

(Projected: A Toni Gayle Comic Book cover)

JANICE
Sure, when she was a detective. I knew I had to get out when it turned into a romance book.

CRANDALL
A ROMANCE? Yeah, I don't know about that.

(Projected: The infamous panel from POPULAR TEEN-AGERS #6 where the coach slaps Butch Dykeman's ass)

JANICE
SOMEBODY was having a laugh. "Toni Gay" and her new boyfriend "Butch Dykeman."

CRANDALL
They're comic book men. Never underestimate the giggle factor.

JANICE
Yeah, and I love it until the joke's on me. I just couldn't go back to the teenybopper stuff. On the upside? I get to ink over Reed Crandall.

CRANDALL
That's ridiculous. I'm a jobber just like you, no need to blow up my skirt. Er...I mean...

JANICE
(Laughs) Now don't get dirty with me, Reed.

CRANDALL
I didn't mean any...

JANICE
All of you guys are so laissez-faire about the work.

(She walks over to CRANDALL's drafting table, and marvels at the page he's working on)

JANICE
This work, THIS WORK! YOUR work? It's as good as anything published anywhere! Sure and confident lines, dynamic and exciting compositions. I wish I could draw like you.

CRANDALL
Janice, you can.

JANICE
I know can draw, but you're my favorite artist, Reed Crandall.

CRANDALL
Drawing Blackhawk? It's a job, it ain't art. I don't kid myself.

JANICE
You're wrong, Reed.

CRANDALL
Nothing like my mother reading Ladies' Home Journal and calling to tell me she's ashamed of me.

JANICE
Who cares about that old fart Wertham.

CRANDALL
What about Kefavuver and Hendrickson?

JANICE
What are you talking about?

CRANDALL
The delinquency hearings?

(CRANDALL *pulls a page from his papers, and hands it to her*)

CRANDALL
...Y'know, it's probably nothing. Here. I want you to have this.

JANICE
The splash page from the last issue?

CRANDALL
Yeah. I want you to have it.

JANICE
Oh Reed! It's gorgeous!

(*She leaps up and hugs him. Unseen to both of them, BUSY ARNOLD, the publisher of Quality Comics enters. He is dressed in a very natty suit and well-groomed*)

BUSY
Hey now! I don't pay you for that kind of shenanigans!!

(*JANICE very quickly releases CRANDALL and retreats to her desk*)

JANICE
I'm sorry, Mister Arnold. We were just...Reed gave me one of his pages...

BUSY
Janice, please...call me Busy. How are we doing on the next thrilling adventure of the Blackhawk squadron!? Hawk-a-a-a!!

CRANDALL
It'll be done.

JANICE
No thanks to me.

BUSY
What's that?

CRANDALL
It's no big deal.

JANICE
I ruined one of Reed's pages.

BUSY
What?

(She shows BUSY the page with a large smear of ink)

BUSY
Woof! No saving that.

JANICE
It's my fault.

BUSY
You'll have to re-draw it, looks like.

CRANDALL
No problem. Quick fix.

BUSY
Crandall...You make sure you turn in your voucher for this page twice.

JANICE
You can dock me, Mister Arnold.

BUSY
Are you kidding? *(To CRANDALL)* Is she kidding?

CRANDALL
I don't think she's kidding.

BUSY
Nobody, and I mean NOBODY, does work for Busy Arnold without a fair paycheck. Tell you what! Reed, you and Janice here can join me at The Stork Club tonight!

JANICE
Oh I don't know...

BUSY
NO EXCUSES! This is my treat. Run home and get

your prettiest dress, and Reed, get your nicest suit. We're going to do the town.

CRANDALL
All right, sir.

BUSY
Busy! BUSY!! No sir, no Mister Arnold, just Busy! Six PM! I'll have a car to take us over to the club.

(BUSY begins to make his way out)

JANICE
I'm not sure.

BUSY
What did I say, Janice?

JANICE
No excuses.

BUSY
Exactly. Quality Comics, AND Busy Arnold, hold the morale of their artists to be of the highest priority.

(He ducks out the door, then suddenly reappears)

BUSY
For God's sake, just accept it!

(With a laugh and a wink, he exits)

CRANDALL
I used to try to argue with him. It's useless.

(Lights shift to black)

SCENE SEVEN

(WERTHAM steps out of the darkness)

WERTHAM
Rub-a-dub-dub, three degenerates go to the club!! One
with a pencil, one with a brush, and the third a gent who
might have a bit of a crush!

(WERTHAM cackles. Then composes himself)

WERTHAM
Only someone ignorant of the fundamentals of the
psychopathology of sex can fail to realize a subtle
atmosphere of homoeroticism which pervades the
adventures of the mature "Batman" and his young friend
"Robin." They are Bruce Wayne and "Dick" Grayson.
They live in sumptuous quarters, with beautiful flowers
in large vases. Batman is sometimes shown in a dressing
gown, reclining, jacket off, collar open. The boy sitting
next to him, his hand on his "friend's" arm. It is like a
wish dream of two homosexuals living together.

(Lights shift to the afternoon light of MATT BAKER's

bedroom. ARCHER ST JOHN lies across the bed, naked under a sheet, as BAKER enters from the bathroom)

ST JOHN
Can't we stay here forever?

BAKER
The boys back at the office would eventually start wondering, and, sooner or later, so would your wife.

ST JOHN
Ah, to hell with her.

(ST JOHN pulls BAKER down on the bed with him)

ST JOHN
She needs my money, and she needs to look respectable.

(They kiss)

BAKER
Respectable? Sounds pretty damn dull.

ST JOHN
Utterly.

(Another kiss)

ST JOHN
I love the way you taste.

BAKER
So you tell me.

ST JOHN
I don't really need to go back to work.

BAKER
Yeah, but I do.

ST JOHN
I go way back with Victor Fox, he owes me one or two.

I can run interference for you.

BAKER
Oh, THAT would be great.

(ST JOHN pulls at BAKER)

ST JOHN
C'mon...

BAKER
There's enough office rumor as it is.

ST JOHN
Does that bother you?

BAKER
I don't need the attention.

ST JOHN
I thought you liked attention?

BAKER
Yours, not Wertham's. I gotta go. The Phantom Lady isn't going to draw herself.

(ST JOHN throws back the covers from over his body)

ST JOHN
She may have nicer tits than I do, but I think you like this more.

BAKER
(Chuckles) You're incorrigible.

ST JOHN
You worry too much.

(BAKER flips the covers back over St John's naked body)

BAKER
You should probably worry more.

ST JOHN
Wertham'll blow over. Why don't you write a letter to the editor, if you're worried?

BAKER
I would guess one from a respected, white publisher might have more impact than from a Black cheesecake artist with a...discrete private life.

ST JOHN
I want more of you.

BAKER
Saint John escapes again!...Later. Have I ever let you down?

ST JOHN
I think I'm still up...

(He starts to pull back the sheet again. BAKER stops him)

BAKER
Funny. Did that line work on Marion McDermott?

ST JOHN
Who?

BAKER
Don't be a liar, Archer.

ST JOHN
Ah, ppffft! She's nothing.

(ST JOHN reaches for a whiskey bottle and pours a drink)

BAKER
What about Lily Renée? She told me you chased her around a desk.

ST JOHN
You talk to the girls too much.

BAKER
They like me. And you, clearly, like them.

(*ST JOHN takes a swig*)

ST JOHN
Jealousy is not a good look on you, Matt.

BAKER
Archer, I am not jealous.

ST JOHN
How can I deny the world all of this?

(*He displays himself. BAKER slips on his jacket, and gathers his valise*)

BAKER
Lock up when you leave.

ST JOHN
Are you mad at me?

(*BAKER takes ST JOHN's face in his hands*)

BAKER
I think you are a beautiful soul, and being here with you is wonderful. I also think you care more about yourself than other people.

(*Another kiss. ST JOHN grabs BAKER so he can't pull away*)

ST JOHN
Maybe, but what if I made you my art director?

BAKER
Are you serious?

ST JOHN
As a heart attack.

(A deep kiss, which is interrupted by a knock at the door. BAKER starts to pull back)

ST JOHN
Ignore it.

(ST JOHN tries to re-start the kiss)

BAKER
Down, boy.

CONNIE *(off stage)*
Matt!? Are you in there!?

BAKER
Oh boy.

ST JOHN
Who is it?

BAKER
A girl.

ST JOHN
Oh ho! Shoe's on the other foot, now.

BAKER
You wish. Get in the bathroom.

ST JOHN
You want me to hide in the bathroom?

BAKER
Jesus, Archer. Don't make this difficult.

(ST JOHN gathers the sheets and heads toward the bathroom)

ST JOHN
You're going to owe me for this, Matty.

(He pauses to grab his bottle, then slips out of sight)

ST JOHN
Gonna need this.

(*BAKER shuts the door behind ST JOHN, and moves to the hall door*)

CONNIE (*off stage*)
I can hear you moving around in there, Baker!

(*BAKER opens the door*)

BAKER
What is it, Connie?

(*CONNIE breezes into the apartment*)

CONNIE
What took you so long?

BAKER
(*Sighs*) I was in the bathroom.

CONNIE
You take more time in there than I do.

BAKER
What do you need, Connie? I have to get to work.

CONNIE
Not even a hello?

BAKER
Hello, Connie...I have to get to work.

CONNIE
Well, despite your rudeness, I'm still going to ask you to be my date tonight. Lucy got me tickets for Parker and Mingus at The Five Spot.

BAKER
How the hell did you swing that?

CONNIE
Lucy knows people.

BAKER
Is that so?

CONNIE
You've GOT to come Matt! Lord knows those two might kill each other, and then we'll never have another chance.

BAKER
I'll go, but I have to work now.

(*He begins to usher her into the hallway. She holds her ground*)

CONNIE
Oh? Just like that? Out the door?

(*He winces and rubs his chest*)

CONNIE
Are you OK?

BAKER
Heartburn, don't worry about it.

CONNIE
I got us tickets to see Misters Charlie Parker and Mingus, and you just shove me out the door? Not even a kiss?

(*Matt kisses her*)

CONNIE
That's better. Now, you go work. Pick me up at seven. Dinner is on you.

(*They exit into the hall. The bathroom door opens, and ST JOHN emerges with his bottle. He plops onto the bed, and takes a swig*)

ST JOHN
You enjoy that show, Matty.

(*Lights shift*)

Scene Eight

(WERTHAM steps back out of the darkness)

WERTHAM
Well, well, well, Mister Baker. Matt be nimble, Matt be quick! His boyfriend's in the bathroom, and he needs to be slick!

(WERTHAM winks)

WERTHAM
We have talked with publishers, writers, artists. Some of them were very co-operative, especially when they talked about firms other than their own. "Those OTHER fellows, they know exactly what they are doing, I don't know how they can look at themselves in the mirror!"

(Lights shift to GAINES' office. FELDSTEIN and GAINES are meeting with JACK DAVIS, a "southern gentleman," and one of their top artists)

DAVIS
It's all so gruesome.

FELDSTEIN
It's not like the guy doesn't deserve it, Jack.

GAINES
True enough! He's a cold-blooded murderer!

DAVIS
It's just...to have the name Jack Davis, MY name, on such an ugly thing.

FELDSTEIN
It's far from ugly...well, I mean, it is...but it's SUPPOSED to be!

GAINES
Ugly or not, THIS is what the kids are buying! We're setting the tone for the whole damn industry!

FELDSTEIN
What Bill is trying to say...

GAINES
Hell, at least we let you put your name on it, Jack!

(SHIRLEY enters)

SHIRLEY
You needed something?

GAINES
Take these over to Marie for coloring.

(SHIRLEY looks at the drawings)

(Projected: Page Seven, Panel two of "Foul Play," with the pitcher preparing to throw a severed head to a batter swinging a severed leg, and a catcher wearing the victim's torso as a chest protector)

SHIRLEY
You people are sick.

FELDSTEIN
(Laughs) Shirley, c'mon! It's just a baseball game!

SHIRLEY
Is that a severed head?

GAINES
It's the ball!

(GAINES and FELDSTEIN laugh)

DAVIS
I think maybe I should withdraw. I'm sorry, Shirley.

GAINES
It's a horror comic! This is what we do, here.

FELDSTEIN
It's not the worst thing we've ever published, by a long shot.

GAINES
(To SHIRLEY) Don't be so high and mighty, I saw you laughing at the one where the old couple murders all the traveling salesmen with their own products.

FELDSTEIN
Which you drew, Jack.

DAVIS
Don't remind me.

(SHIRLEY gathers the boards, and begins to head out)

SHIRLEY
I'll drop these off, and then go vomit.

(She exits)

FELDSTEIN
Jack, I understand how you feel. Go talk to Marie Severin. She can take some of the edge off it with the coloring.

GAINES
But not too much!!

FELDSTEIN
Calm down, Bill.

DAVIS
I'll drop by her desk.

GAINES
What the hell are we doing here, if we're not freaking people out!?

(FELDSTEIN walks DAVIS to the door, and DAVIS exits. FELDSTEIN turns back to GAINES)

GAINES
What the hell is wrong with people?! Jack Davis knows damn well what we do here. He got his check. He knew what he was getting into! I say...let 'im stew!

FELDSTEIN
Bill, you gotta work with people, here. They're on edge with all the press about Wertham.

(Lights shift. WERTHAM appears)

WERTHAM
What can I say? The camera loves me.

(WERTHAM slips into the darkness, lights shift back to the office)

GAINES
Don't mention that ghoul.

FELDSTEIN
He's making a lot of noise.

GAINES
I thought it was going to be smooth sailing after that crap with Bradbury.

FELDSTEIN
Well, you were stealing his stories.

GAINES
I can't remember everything I've read!

FELDSTEIN
Only one of the most famous authors in America...

GAINES
Never mind that! I paid him, and now we're legit.

FELDSTEIN
Getting caught tends to right the scales.

GAINES
Look, are you on my side, or not?!

FELDSTEIN
Bill, I am ALWAYS on your side. I'm just giving you the business.

GAINES
I don't need your "business," Al.

FELDSTEIN
(Chuckles) Yeah, ya do.

(The door bangs open, and LYLE STUART, the EC Business Manager, bursts in)

STUART
IT'S A BUST!!

GAINES
What the hell?

FELDSTEIN
Are you kidding?

STUART
The cops are here! They want the president of the company!

GAINES
What!?!

FELDSTEIN
Why?

(GAINES grabs STUART)

GAINES
You have to do something, Lyle! I can't go to jail! They'll eat me alive in there!

STUART
What are we going to do?

GAINES
Why are you asking me? YOU'RE the one with the rap sheet!

STUART
When I was FIFTEEN!

FELDSTEIN
(To STUART) Ok, Stuart, obviously our fearless leader has gone bye-bye...

STUART
No kidding!

FELDSTEIN
Calm down, Lyle! Take a breath. You're the business manager, what do we do?

STUART
Well, if it's an obscenity thing, we should be fine as long as we don't sell them a book.

FELDSTEIN
Well, that's easy enough.

(SHIRLEY enters)

SHIRLEY
Do you have a lawyer?

GAINES
Of course, why?

SHIRLEY
That cop asked to buy a copy of "Panic," so I sold it to them.

(Beat)

STUART
Oh shit.

GAINES
I need to get out of here!

FELDSTEIN
That's not even a horror book! What the Hell?

SHIRLEY
They're taking me down to the station for booking. I told them I needed to get my coat and purse. I just want to make damn sure I am going to get overtime for this.

GAINES
What!? I don't know...

SHIRLEY
ACT LIKE A MAN FOR CHRISTSAKES, GAINES!!!

(GAINES stops dead)

GAINES
Yes, ma'am.

SHIRLEY
Are. YOU. Going. To PAY. ME. For this?

(Beat)

GAINES
Well, yes, of course.

SHIRLEY
Great. I'm going to get my coat, and they can cuff me. I am going to expect someone at the station with bail money. *(She turns and begins to exit)* It's like these people don't even know how to run a business. *(Exits)*

FELDSTEIN
An issue of Panic? Really?

STUART
It's the Night Before Christmas thing. When you defile a holiday classic, some people get up in arms.

FELDSTEIN
It's a joke! It's a humor mag.

STUART
Not a creature was stirring, because they were dead on meat hooks?

(Projected: Page one, panel three of "The Night Before Christmas" from Panic Comics #1, with the aforementioned imagery, and other sight gags)

FELDSTEIN
Yeah, including an elephant. The art was ridiculous!

STUART
Apparently, the cops see it differently. I'm going to go bail out Shirley.

(STUART exits. GAINES smacks his head down on his desktop)

GAINES
I finally get to where I'm doing something I actually enjoy, despite my damn father...What are we going to do Al?

FELDSTEIN
I mean, this sort of thing usually blows over. The publicity can't hurt, right?

(Lights shift. WERTHAM appears and laughs)

WERTHAM
What's the saying in English? "The best laid plans of mice and men?"

(WERTHAM holds up a dead mouse by its tail, much like the panel we saw)

WERTHAM
Still not stirring....

(More laughter, almost cackling. The lights fade to black...)

Scene Nine

(Projected: The Seal of the US Senate)

(SENATOR ROBERT C HENDRICKSON steps into the light)

(Projected: SENATOR ROBERT C HENDRICKSON)

HENDRICKSON
The United States Subcommittee on Juvenile Delinquency, of which I am the Chairman, is going into the problem of horror and crime comic books...

(SENATOR ESTES KEFAUVER steps into the light, upstaging HENDRICKSON, who notes his appearance, annoyed, but continues)

HENDRICKSON
We are not a committee of blue-nosed censors. We are fully aware of the long, hard, bitter fight that has been waged to achieve and preserve the freedom of the press, as well as the other freedoms in our Bill of Rights which we cherish in America...

(KEFAUVER steps in front of HENDRICKSON)

(Projected: SENATOR ESTES KEFAUVER - FUTURE PRESIDENTIAL CANDIDATE)

KEFAUVER
I want to compliment Chairman Hendrickson on a very excellent statement of the purposes of this subcommittee. I would emphasize that this nation DOES have a postal statute which prohibits the using of mails for the distribution of indecent and scurrilous literature.

(HENDRICKSON slips back past KEFAUVER)

HENDRICKSON
That is certainly correct, Senator Kefauver.

(KEFAUVER sidesteps him again)

KEFAUVER
I think it is also important to note a report from DIRECTOR J EDGAR HOOVER shows that crime had gone up twenty percent, particularly in burglary and auto theft. A large part of these crimes committed by juveniles.

HENDRICKSON
I would certainly concur that...

(HENDRICKSON attempts to take the front again, but KEFAUVER blocks him)

KEFAUVER
As the...Chairman...said, we do not have all the answers, but we are here to determine what effect of causation crime and horror comics do have.

(HENDRICKSON makes a big move and gets around KEFAUVER)

HENDRICKSON

The Senator from Tennessee is entirely correct and
THE CHAIR wishes to congratulate and commend the
Senator for his contribution.

*(KEFAUVER steps out with a big, big smile, waving.
Flashbulbs, and then fade to black)*

SCENE TEN

(WERTHAM emerges from the darkness)

WERTHAM
Isn't it wonderful when a serious work of psychological research can have such an important impact on our society?

(He holds up a first edition copy of SEDUCTION OF THE INNOCENT)

(Projected: The cover of SEDUCTION OF THE INNOCENT)

WERTHAM
With the release of this book, we reveal the results of SEVEN YEARS of research into the effects of comic books on today's youth. Many illustrations showing excessive violence, sex, sadism and torture are shown! Seduction of the Innocent by Doctor Fredric Wertham, MD. Available for ONLY FOUR DOLLARS at a bookstore near you!

(Lights shift and WERTHAM disappears. We are back

in GAINES' office. STUART and FELDSTEIN are watching GAINES pace with manic energy, swigging from a coke bottle)

STUART
This is a BAD idea.

FELDSTEIN
Bill, I think maybe you should lay off the soda.

GAINES
Whatdoyamean?

(GAINES pops a pill and washes it back with the pop)

FELDSTEIN
Maybe the pills, too.

GAINES
What the hell are you talking about? It's just Dexedrine. My doctor gave it to me.

(GAINES opens another bottle and takes a different pill)

STUART
And what are THOSE?

GAINES
Don't worry about it. Over-the-counter stuff.

FELDSTEIN
How many have you taken?

GAINES
I have to be sharp tomorrow! I have to be ready! I am not going to let that Kefauver do a hatchet job on me!

FELDSTEIN
Wasn't the ad enough? ·

GAINES
They're trying to shut us down, Al! I'm going to fight

back with everything I have.

STUART
Well, that didn't win you any friends on the committee.

GAINES
It was the truth!

(GAINES picks up a comic flips to the ad, and reads it)

GAINES
"Here in America, we can STILL publish comic magazines, newspapers, and the Bible! We don't HAVE to send them to a censor first, Not YET! But there are some in America who would LIKE to censor and suppress comics. It isn't that they don't like comics for THEM! They don't like them for YOU!" *(Throws the issue down)* What the hell is wrong with that?

FELDSTEIN
Well, a couple lines later you infer an entire Senate subcommittee is made up of Communists.

GAINES
If the shoe fits!

STUART
Good Lord, Bill.

FELDSTEIN
Bill, this is nuts. I told you weeks ago not to testify.

GAINES
I volunteered!

FELDSTEIN
I know! I still can't figure out why.

GAINES
Somebody has to defend us.

STUART
You look like you're in great shape for it.

FELDSTEIN
What is it, Bill? What are you trying to prove?

GAINES
I can answer their questions! I just need to go down there and say my piece. They'll understand. Everything will be fine. I just need a good opening statement.

FELDSTEIN
We know.

STUART
You've called us every night this week with a new version.

GAINES
You guys have to HELP ME!!

STUART
Fine!!

(STUART marches behind GAINES' desk, pulls the typewriter over, and sits)

STUART
Look at me Bill!

(GAINES turns his focus to STUART)

STUART
I'm a United States Senator, and I'm wondering if I should pass a law to put you out of business. Is there anything you'd like to say to me?

(GAINES stops, the lights shift and he begins to speak as the stage transitions)

SCENE ELEVEN

(The Senate Committee Room. KEFAUVER and HENDRICKSON take elevated seats looking down at GAINES)

GAINES

My name is William Gaines. I am a graduate of New York University, with qualifications to teach high school. I am also a comic book publisher. My group is known as Entertaining Comics. My father helped found the comic magazine industry he two decades ago, and was proud to bring enjoyment to millions of people. Weaning hundreds of thousands of children from pictures to the printed word. Stirring their imagination with millions of hours of entertainment while giving them an outlet for their problems and frustrations.

(At this point, GAINES will slowly begin to slip into a weird post-Dexedrine state, licking his lips strangely and rarely looking up from his prepared statement. Almost like a balloon running out of air)

GAINES

I was the first publisher in these United States to publish

horror comics. I am responsible. I started them. Some may not like them.

(GAINES mumbles unintelligibly to himself)

GAINES
That is a matter of personal taste. It would be just as difficult to explain the harmless thrill of a horror story to a Doctor Wertham as it would be to explain the sublimity of love to a frigid old maid.

(GAINES pulls at his tie, and wipes sweat from his brow with his sleeve)

GAINES
I am proud of the comics I publish. We use the best writers, the finest artists; we spare nothing to make each magazine, each story, each page, a work of art.

(GAINES coughs, and sniffles in an odd way)

GAINES
The truth is that delinquency is the product of real environment, in which the child lives, and not the fiction he reads.

(GAINES head slips downward, and he is oddly staring at a point on the table in front of him)

GAINES
What are we afraid of? We think our children are so evil, simple minded, that it takes a story of murder to set them to murder, a story of robbery to set them to robbery?

HENDRICKSON
Is the sole test of what you would put into your magazine whether it sells? Is there any limit you can think of that you would not put in a magazine because you thought a child should not see or read about it?

(GAINES continues to stare at the point on the table, only in brief moments looking up toward the Senators)

GAINES

No, I wouldn't say there was any limit for the reason you outlined. My only limits are bounds of good taste.

HENDRICKSON

Then you think a child cannot in any way, in any way, shape, or manner, be hurt by anything a child reads or sees? There would be no limit to what you put in the magazines?

GAINES

Only within the bounds of good taste...what I consider good taste.

(KEFAUVER holds up a copy of CRIME SUSPENSTORIES #22, with a man holding a bloody axe and a woman's severed head)

(Projected: The cover of CRIME SUSPENSTORIES #22)

KEFAUVER

Here is your May 22 issue. This seems to be a man with a bloody axe holding a woman's head up which has been severed from her body...Do you think THAT is in good taste?

GAINES

Yes, sir, I do, for the cover of a horror comic.

(Another cough and sniffle)

GAINES

A cover in bad taste, for example, might be defined as holding the head a little higher so that the neck could be seen dripping blood from it and moving the body over a little further so that the neck of the body could be seen....to be bloody.

KEFAUVER
You have blood coming out of her mouth!

GAINES
...A little.

(HENDRICKSON holds up a copy of the "Are You a
Red Dupe?" feature)

HENDRICKSON
Mister Gaines, do you know anything about this sheet
called, "Are you a Red dupe?"

GAINES
Yes, sir I wrote it.

HENDRICKSON
Do you believe that anybody who is anxious to destroy
comics is a Communist?

GAINES
I don't believe it says that.

(Projected; The EC Comics "Are You a Red Dupe"
editorial)

HENDRICKSON
It says it right here; "The Group Most Anxious To
Destroy Comics Are The Communists" exclamation
point, no less.

GAINES
True, but not anybody, just the group most anxious.

KEFAUVER
Mr Gaines, I had heard your father really did not have
horror and crime comics. When he had the business he
printed things that were really funny, and stories of the
Bible, but you are the one who started out this crime
and horror business.

GAINES
I did not start crime, I started horror.

(*KEFAUVER waves VAULT OF HORROR #30, with a severed arm dangling from a subway ring*)

(*Projected: The cover of VAULT OF HORROR #30*)

KEFAUVER
Do you let children in your own family, nieces, nephews, read your magazines?

GAINES
My family has no children.

(*The lights shift to black*)

SCENE TWELVE

(WERTHAM appears out of the darkness. He holds a book, as if the Bible, and raises his right hand)

WERTHAM

I swear to tell the truth, the whole truth, and nothing but the truth... *(Chuckles)* I have testified six times under oath on the psychiatric analysis of what constitutes obscenity. Pointing out that a picture of a nude girl could be the opposite of obscene. Compared to a girl in a brassiere and panties about to be tied up, gagged, tortured, set on fire, sold as a slave, chained, whipped, choked, raped, thrown to wild animals or crocodiles, forced to her knees, strangled, torn apart and so on.

(He raises the book, revealing it to be THE SEDUCTION OF THE INNOCENT again)

WERTHAM

Nothing like a Congressional investigation to drive book sales.

(The lights shift, and JANICE and CRANDALL are

watching the hearings on a TV in the Quality Comics bullpen)

JANICE
What the heck is wrong with him?

CRANDALL
He's a weird guy, Janice.

JANICE
Well, yeah. Everybody talks about that, but...I mean, he looks drugged.

CRANDALL
Who knows what the heck they do over there? You've seen those disgusting books. And our jobs may be in THAT guy's hands.

JANICE
Disgusting? You can't really think that.

CRANDALL
You ever see the one about the old couple murdering door-to-door salesmen with their own products? Meat slicers and the like?

JANICE
Yeah, I did. It was pretty funny.

CRANDALL
Waitaminute...what did he just say? A severed head is in good taste?!

(He throws up his hands and marches back toward his drawing table)

CRANDALL
Guess I'd better start getting the ol' portfolio together.

JANICE
Is everything always worst case scenario with you?

BUSY *(off stage)*
That Goddamn fool!! Goddamn stupid fool!!

(BUSY bursts into the bullpen)

BUSY
I told him not to do it, marched right into the lions den!

CRANDALL
Gaines is a weird guy.

BUSY
Trying to play hero, like a fucking moron!

(He notices JANICE)

BUSY
Oh, sorry Janice, I shouldn't...

JANICE
Like I fucking care.

CRANDALL
EXCUSE ME, but what are we going to do?

(BUSY grabs his coat and hat)

BUSY
I'm going to talk with Goldwater, St John, Donenfeld, Goodman, and whoever the else I can find. We have to figure out what to do about this shitstorm Max Gaines' idiot son unleashed.

(He exits, slamming the door. Beat. The door re-opens and BUSY's head appears)

BUSY
Sorry, Janice...I just...

JANICE
I've heard "shit" before, too, Busy.

(BUSY nods and exits)

CRANDALL
I'd still get my portfolio in order, Janice.

(She looks at him. The lights shift)

SCENE THIRTEEN

(Lights shift to BAKER's apartment, CONNIE is laying upon a couch, while BAKER sketches her)

BAKER
Can you drop the robe just a little, Connie?

CONNIE
Oh, do you want to see more?

BAKER
It would be better for the composition.

CONNIE
Is that so?

BAKER
The lines would be more organic.

(She drops the robe a bit, exposing the swell of her breast)

CONNIE
Like this?

(He analyzes her with a look)

BAKER
That works.

(His pencil works on the paper)

CONNIE
Maybe I should take it off completely?

BAKER
If you'd be comfortable.

(She stands and walks to him, the robe slipping down more)

CONNIE
Maybe YOU should get comfortable.

(He looks up at her, and the door bursts open, and GUISTO bursts in)

GUISTO
Matt! Holy shit, are you watching TV!?!

(CONNIE screams and rushes into the bathroom)

BAKER
Frank, I told you to knock...

GUISTO
There's no time for that! Haven't you been watching the hearings?

BAKER
What are you talking about?

GUISTO
Gaines is on TV selling us all down the river!

BAKER
Bill Gaines? From EC?

GUISTO
Yeah! He's in the middle of the hearing acting like he's been snortin' out of the wrong bottle.

BAKER
Maybe he has.

GUISTO
They said he ASKED to testify.

BAKER
He's a weird guy, Frank.

(GUISTO stops, and looks at the bathroom door)

GUISTO
Waitaminute...Was that a woman?

BAKER
Yeah.

GUISTO
Why's there a naked woman in your apartment? Oh, man...wait. Could that work for me?

BAKER
Not likely. She's modeling for me. *(He starts putting his supplies away)*

GUISTO
Yeeeah. I tried that one, didn't work.

(The bathroom door opens, and CONNIE re-enters, fully dressed)

CONNIE
Who the HELL are YOU!?!

BAKER
Connie, this is my best friend, Frank Guisto.

CONNIE
Why did he barge in?

GUISTO
There's these Senate hearings going on...

BAKER
The juvenile delinquency hearings.

CONNIE
Why does that give breaking and entering here the right to see me naked?

GUISTO
They're coming after us! They're coming after comics!

CONNIE
Well, maybe you deserve it!

BAKER
This is how I make my living.

CONNIE
Matt, you're so talented, you can do so much better than this! I read that article in Ladies' Home Journal. They're almost calling it pornography!

GUISTO
Lady, you were the one parading around half naked.

CONNIE
Was I talking to you?!

GUISTO
Hey, this is MY job, too. Just like him.

BAKER
I like my work. I like the people I work with.

GUISTO
And we like him, too.

(CONNIE pulls BAKER away for a bit of privacy)

CONNIE
You could get a job teaching, or you could work for an advertising agency. We could be married, have a little house...

BAKER
Connie, I...

GUISTO
We like him the way he is.

CONNIE
This is none of your business!

BAKER
Connie, I think...

CONNIE
You'd better think, Mister Matt Baker! Because I'm not going to wait around for you forever.

BAKER
Connie, don't...

CONNIE
You just think about it!

(She exits, slamming the door)

GUISTO
That went well.

BAKER
Shut up, Frank.

(BAKER winces a bit, and rubs his chest)

GUISTO
OK, but both of us need to figure out what we're going to do if Gaines just screwed the entire industry.

(Lights shift to black)

END OF ACT ONE

ACT II

Scene One

(WERTHAM once again steps out of the darkness)

WERTHAM

Welcome Back, meine freunde! I hope you had time for a nice cigarette or bit of candy! I receive letters and inquires from all over the country, expressing a similar refrain, "We who care about such things feel so helpless. Who thinks these comic books are good?" The answer, is, of course, simple, the comic book industry! There was the possible remedy that the publishers could set right their own house.

(WERTHAM produces a gleaming axe, dripping with blood)

WERTHAM

Can we trust the hand that is in the cookie jar? Or is it better to lop it off?

(He fades into the shadows as we shift to a meeting room. GAINES, STUART and FELDSTEIN sit at one end of the table, while JOHN GOLDWATER, BUSY

ARNOLD, ARCHER ST JOHN sit opposite. One man sits in shadow behind GOLDWATER's group)

GOLDWATER
WHAT THE HELL WERE YOU THINKING!?!?!

GAINES
I was trying...

BUSY
You dropped an A–Bomb on the whole damn business, Gaines!

GOLDWATER
Just when we needed to lay low, you had to go in there grandstanding.

ST JOHN
Do we all have to yell so much?

GOLDWATER
I'm not concerned with your hangover, Archer.

ST JOHN
Clearly.

BUSY
You need to cut back, St John.

ST JOHN
Mind your own business, Busy.

GOLDWATER
Can we please focus on the bigger screw-up in the room?

STUART
Mister Gaines was trying to defend our industry.

GOLDWATER
And managed to nail the coffin shut!

GAINES
Look, what happened, happened.

BUSY
What the hell were you on?

FELDSTEIN
It was a sugar crash.

(Beat)

GOLDWATER
You have GOT to be kidding.

STUART
You wouldn't believe how many Cokes he drank.

ST JOHN
Even I'm not going to believe he was under the influence of soda pop.

FELDSTEIN
You know what they say about glass houses, Archer?

BUSY
At least he didn't screw the pooch on national TV!

GAINES
Look! I'm sorry that I didn't come off as well as I wanted to...

GOLDWATER
What were you going for? Richard Hauptmann?

GAINES
...But we can't just lie down and let them bury us! That's why I called this meeting. We need to stick together and protect ourselves.

GOLDWATER
Self-regulation.

GAINES
No! We just need the political clout to push back on Wertham and Kefauver and the rest of those bastards.

BUSY
They're not going to leave us alone unless we crack down ourselves.

GOLDWATER
They're already moving in Houston and Oklahoma City to ban us, legally.

GAINES
It'll never stand up in court. If we get our own legal team...

BUSY
Good God, Bill! Have you seen the burnings?

GAINES
What are you talking about?

GOLDWATER
Are you kidding?

STUART
(To GAINES) I tried to warn you on the way over.

FELDSTEIN
(To STUART) I told you not to let him stop for that sandwich.

STUART
He said he was hungry! I didn't want a repeat...

FELDSTEIN
He doesn't hear ANYTHING if he's eating.

STUART
All our budget meetings are over lunch!

FELDSTEIN
Yeah. I've been trying to wave you off of those for the last year and a half. *(Beat)* You're not the best listener, either.

GAINES
What the hell is he talking about?

STUART
They're burning comics, Bill.

GAINES
What? The government?

FELDSTEIN
People, Bill. All over. Parents, teachers, churches.

GOLDWATER
Kids, Gaines. Kids are burning our comics.

GAINES
That's insane.

BUSY
Lot of that going around.

GOLDWATER
Two thousand books in Binghamton.

BUSY
A Goddamn Girl Scout troop in Missouri! They had a trial! The flames were twenty-five feet high.

GAINES
I didn't...

GOLDWATER
And you waltzed in there and damn near passed out in front of a Presidential candidate!

(Beat)

ST JOHN
He hasn't announced...

GOLDWATER
...LIKELY Presidential candidate!

GAINES
All of this, all of this, just proves that we need to work
together.

GOLDWATER
What we need to do, is rein it in.

GAINES
What does that mean?

BUSY
We need to get things under control.

FELDSTEIN
What do you mean, "under control?"

GOLDWATER
I think...Well, we'll let Judge Murphy explain.

GAINES
Who?

(The shadowy figure gets up and walks out from behind
GOLDWATER's group. This is JUDGE CHARLES
MURPHY)

MURPHY
Mister Gaines, my name is JUDGE Charles Murphy.

STUART
Are we supposed to bow, or something?

MURPHY
That's very cute, Mister...Stuart? Lyle Stuart, if I'm not
mistaken.

FELDSTEIN
You're obviously making a point, just do it.

MURPHY
Mister Stuart has quite the criminal record, gentleman.

GOLDWATER
Is that so?

STUART
What the hell are you talking about? My juvenile record?

MURPHY
I think that might be relevant, Mister Stuart, seeing as how we're dealing with an investigation of juvenile delinquency. Misters Goldwater, St John, Arnold, myself, as well as most of the rest of the major publishers, have been discussing how to rectify the fallout from this recent public outcry, as well as, it goes without saying, your testimony.

GAINES
So you've been talking behind my back.

GOLDWATER
Let him speak, Gaines!

MURPHY
It was an excellent opportunity for us when you arranged this meeting, and we certainly thank you for renting the room.

GAINES
You're welcome.

FELDSTEIN
Get to the point. What's the deal?

MURPHY
If we fail to take action, we may find ourselves forced into government, either national or local, regulation.

STUART
We actually don't know that.

MURPHY
The best option is for the industry, you gentlemen, to regulate yourselves, rather than some outside force motivated by public over-reaction.

FELDSTEIN
And all of you AREN'T motivated by public over-reaction?

STUART
They haven't even suggested legislation.

MURPHY
Gentlemen, I can guarantee that the Senators are considering it.

GAINES
The way that bastard Kefauver wants to be President, I wouldn't put it past him.

GOLDWATER
The Judge and I have a plan.

MURPHY
A regulatory organization for the industry. I suggest "The Comics Code Authority."

(MURPHY reveals a large easel board with the CCA logo)

(Projected: The Comics Code Authority Logo)

FELDSTEIN
Who's "the authority?"

BUSY
We hired Judge Murphy. He's going to administrate.

GAINES, FELDSTEIN AND STUART
THIS guy?

GOLDWATER
He's an honored New York Magistrate.

FELDSTEIN
(To MURPHY) You ever done anything creative?

MURPHY
I think that's irrelevant.

GAINES
I beg to differ.

MURPHY
I have drafted a list of prohibitions and guidelines that
should be placed in effect as soon as possible.

*(He pulls out several sheets of paper and hands a copy
to each man. GAINES doesn't look at it, STUART and
FELDSTEIN begin to read)*

GAINES
Are we not going to vote on this?

BUSY
We already have.

GOLDWATER
Unanimously.

STUART
(Looking up from reading) Now, hold on!

FELDSTEIN
What is this?

MURPHY
The rules that will keep you in business.

FELDSTEIN
This isn't going to work!

STUART

(Reading from the paper) "The letters of the word 'CRIME' on a comics-magazine cover shall never be appreciably greater in dimension than the other words contained in the title..."

FELDSTEIN

(Also reading) "The word 'CRIME' shall never appear alone on a cover. Restraint of the word 'CRIME' in titles or subtitles shall be exercised."

STUART

(Continuing) "No comic magazine shall use the word 'HORROR' or 'TERROR' in its title."

GAINES

You do realize that two of our best-selling books are "Crime SuspenStories" and "Vault of Horror."

MURPHY

You'll have to change them to get Code approval.

GOLDWATER

Or...cancel them.

FELDSTEIN

(Still reading) "All lurid, unsavory, gruesome illustrations shall be eliminated." What the hell are we supposed to use to scare people? Clowns?

(GAINES has picked up the sheet and is now reading)

GAINES

"Divorce shall not be treated humorously nor represented as desirable." You guys would sing a different tune if you met my ex-wife.

MURPHY

That joke would not be allowed.

STUART
(Reading) "Scenes dealing with, or instruments associated with walking dead, torture, vampires and vampirism, ghouls, cannibalism and werewolfism are prohibited."

FELDSTEIN
It's called Lycanthropy.

GAINES
"Policemen, judges, Government officials and respected institutions shall never be presented in such a way as to create disrespect for established authority."

STUART
So satire and humor are out too?

FELDSTEIN
Why not outlaw war stories? That'd kill off the rest of our line.

ST JOHN
Nobody's complaining about the war books.

MURPHY
As long as they meet the rest of the code.

FELDSTEIN
So, poor, brave soldiers marching off to die for the whims of uncaring politicians is OK, as long as we don't, y'know...actually think about what's happening.

GAINES
"Suggestive and salacious illustration or suggestive posture is unacceptable."

STUART
Put away the headlights, Al.

GAINES
You guys don't "get" your audience, do you?

GOLDWATER
I know they're burning my product.

(Beat)

GAINES
I am not going to be part of this.

(GAINES rises and begins packing up)

BUSY
That's a mistake, Bill.

GAINES
Is it?

MURPHY
If the adherence to the Code is not universal, the Government may feel forced to act.

GAINES
It's Goddamn blackmail.

ST JOHN
Can't you just get in line, Bill?

GAINES
Why does that mean I have to shut down most of my line of books? Couldn't be because we're outselling all of you put together!

MURPHY
I have no interest in sales.

GAINES
That's MORE than clear looking at your little "code," here!

BUSY
Calm down, Bill. Your father would've understood.

GOLDWATER
If you hadn't tried to go out there and play hero, you

wouldn't be in this mess, and neither would the rest of us!

(GAINES, FELDSTEIN and STUART begin to march out)

GOLDWATER
Don't you walk out on me, Gaines!

(BILL stops, and turns to the men still seated)

GAINES
THIS IS THE LAST TIME I HOST A MEETING!!!

(The three men from EC exit, and the lights shift)

Scene Two

(*WERTHAM steps out of the darkness*)

WERTHAM
In an issue of a popular comic book there is on the back cover a full-page color picture.

(*Projected: CITATION MISSING*)

WERTHAM
It shows a stalwart youth, nude except for a well-filled loin cloth. The boy has long blonde hair falling over his shoulders and bound with a red ribbon over his forehead. On both wrists are green bracelets, and graceful ribbons twist around his ankles above his bare feet. He wears a bare dagger coquettishly fixed in front of one hip. He has blue eyes and a beautiful suntan. Test subjects described this picture with vague fears that they might be homosexual, which leads to great anguish as these boys usually have no one in whom they feel they can confide.

(*The lights shift. The Offices of ST JOHN press. BAKER*

walks into ARCHER's office)

ST JOHN
Matt! What are you doing here?

BAKER
I was supposed to see you at my apartment the other day.
We were going to talk about that art director job.

ST JOHN
The art director job?

BAKER
I missed you, Archer.

ST JOHN
I miss you too, Matt.

(ARCHER retreats behind his desk)

ST JOHN
Everything's nuts because of that bastard Gaines.

BAKER
You didn't seem all that concerned before.

ST JOHN
Everything was fine before he went out there and embarrassed himself.

BAKER
I think he thought he was doing the right thing.

ST JOHN
What he did was force us all to clean up his mess.

BAKER
This code thing?

*(ARCHER pulls a bottle from his desk, and pours two
glasses as he speaks)*

ST JOHN
Goldwater cooked it up with this Judge he found.

BAKER
And?

ST JOHN
Oh Hell, Matt...Here...

(ARCHER tries to hand BAKER a drink)

BAKER
My doctor told me to cut back. I think a whiskey on the rocks at ten AM on a Tuesday doesn't qualify.

ST JOHN
At least it's not straight.

BAKER
Is that a joke?

(Beat)

ST JOHN
You're a cheesecake artist, Matt. Not to mention our... social activities. I need to be careful for a while.

(ARCHER comes closer, BAKER catches a whiff of his breath)

BAKER
I think what you need is a breath mint.

ST JOHN
Matt, take the drink.

BAKER
No more trips to Stewart's Cafeteria?

(ARCHER drains both drinks)

BAKER
Maybe you should see my doctor.

ST JOHN
I want you. Dammit, Matt.

BAKER
See, I gotta wonder...did you tell Marion McDermott the same thing?

ST JOHN
She's nothing.

BAKER
Lily Renée, then! Are you going to blacklist me, while you still run off to Florida with one of your female staffers when you're bored?

ST JOHN
I'm never bored of you! It's just...

BAKER
An artist known for salacious art, who also happens to be a fairy! That would be a hell of a catch for Judge Charles Murphy, wouldn't it? Wouldn't want that to soil your reputation, would you?

(ARCHER comes closer to him, puts his hand on BAKER's chest)

ST JOHN
I would never...

BAKER
Yeah, yeah, you wouldn't do that.

(He pushes ARCHER's hand away)

ST JOHN
If it wasn't for Gertrude...

BAKER
And suddenly you're concerned about your marriage.

ST JOHN
Matt. Please, please. This mess that Gaines unleashed is
going to take months to untangle. Once things have
calmed down, we can...

BAKER
Stop blaming Gaines for what you're doing!

(Beat)

ST JOHN
Matt, Don't hate me.

(The intercom on ST JOHN's desk buzzes)

SECRETARY *(off stage)*
Mister St John, your wife is here.

ST JOHN
You need to go out the back door.

BAKER
Why should I do that for you?

ST JOHN
I hid in the bathroom for you!

(ARCHER hits his intercom)

ST JOHN
Tell her to give me a moment, Henrietta.

SECRETARY *(off stage)*
She's already on her way.

BAKER
Was it ever a real offer, Archer?

ST JOHN
Please, Matt, go out the back.

BAKER
The Art Director job?

(GERTRUDE ST JOHN enters)

GERTRUDE
I told you to get out of this God-awful business, the ladies at the club can't stop clucking about that idiot on the TV.

ST JOHN
Gaines?

GERTRUDE
I don't know what his name is, but... *(She stops and looks at BAKER)* Is this another of your toys? I had no idea you were trolling...dark waters now.

BAKER
I'm sorry, what?

ST JOHN
This is Matt Baker, Gertrude, one of the best artists in the business.

GERTRUDE
"Artist?"

ST JOHN
He worked on It Rhymes With Lust with Arnold....

GERTRUDE
Oh, I bet he did.

BAKER
I don't have to sit here and listen...

GERTRUDE
I'm sure Archer has made you many promises, Mister... Baker? Was it?

ST JOHN
Gertrude, what can I do for you?

GERTRUDE
If you want to defile yourself all over this city, well, there's not much I can do to stop you. But for God's sake, don't be stupid about it. It's bad enough you work in this vile business, let alone...(Side-eyes BAKER)... Your other obsessions.

ST JOHN
(To BAKER) I told you you should go.

BAKER
Are you going to let her talk that way?

ST JOHN
Matt...I'll call you later.

BAKER
Are you going to let her talk that way TO ME?

(ARCHER is silent)

BAKER
I see.

(BAKER begins to leave, he stops, short of breath, and rubs his chest)

ST JOHN
Matt! Are you OK?

(ST JOHN moves to him. BAKER pushes him away)

BAKER
It's only my heart, Archer.

(BAKER exits. ARCHER turns and looks at GERTRUDE, who smiles. Lights Shift)

SCENE THREE

(Once again, WERTHAM steps from the darkness. Carrying a small, colorful box)

WERTHAM
Poor Mister St John. We often see fearful, insecure men seek the attentions of others to cover their fears of inadequacy. Alas, perhaps Mister Baker's heart...is no longer in it.

(WERTHAM opens the box to reveal a beating heart)

WERTHAM
Cholesterol! It's a killer!

(WERTHAM laughs The Lights shift and JANICE VALLEAU steps through the door into BUSY ARNOLD's office)

JANICE
Busy? You wanted to see me?

BUSY
Janice, come in.

JANICE
Everyone out in the bullpen is paranoid as hell right now.

BUSY
There's a lot of that going around.

JANICE
The Gaines thing, right? He's a weird guy.

BUSY
That's an understatement.

JANICE
Crandall's convinced you're gonna shut the whole thing down, and we're going to be out on the street. He's beside himself out there.

BUSY
I'm sorry.

JANICE
Y'know what would be great right now? We should all go back to the Stork Club! Another night out for the team, something to get our minds off of all this. Some fun!

BUSY
Janice...That's not going to happen.

JANICE
Is business really that bad?...Well, look, it doesn't have to be the Stork Club. Someplace cheaper. Or we can all go dutch! We just need to be a team again.

BUSY
My wife saw the pictures of us at the club.

(Long beat)

BUSY
I'll give you a glowing reference, Janice.

JANICE
Wait, what?

BUSY
This whole thing is a nightmare. Sales are hurting, and I need to cut back somewhere. Frankly, Janice, you know I think you're great, but Reed sells more books than you...and then, well, my wife...

JANICE
So, because your wife doesn't like me, I'm fired?

BUSY
Quite honestly, I don't think my wife likes me much, either.

JANICE
Well, poor you!

BUSY
Please, this is hard enough.

JANICE
Well, I'm SO SORRY it's hard for YOU! I'm the one with my butt on the street.

BUSY
I can call some people. Maybe Goodman's nephew has something at Atlas.

JANICE
Do they have work? I thought he was being paranoid, but the way Crandall tells it, the whole industry's on its last legs!

BUSY
Maybe once the Code calms everything down...

JANICE
I don't give a damn about the code! I thought we were friends, Busy.

BUSY
There's no friends in business, Janice.

(Beat)

JANICE
I'll remember that.

(JANICE exits, slamming the door. BUSY sits quietly as the lights shift)

Scene Four

(WERTHAM, again, emerges from the darkness. He produces a handful of comic books)

WERTHAM
You would not go far wrong if you assumed, after trading and borrowing, that a comic book was read by half a million children, spreading the infection of delinquency. With so many trading hands without payment, the publisher must print about three hundred thousand copies in order to make any kind of profit.

(Lights shift. GAINES' office at EC Comics. GAINES, STUART and FELDSTEIN are having a meeting, the door bursts open and SHIRLEY enters with a large box)

STUART
What the hell?!

GAINES
Shirley, what is this?

SHIRLEY
There's thirty of these in reception. What do you want me to do with them?

FELDSTEIN
What are you talking about?

SHIRLEY
The distributors.

STUART
What about them?

SHIRLEY
They sent these all back.

GAINES
To the office?

(SHIRLEY takes a beat, looks at the box she's holding)

SHIRLEY
Oh, I'm sorry. This is the hair dryer I ordered.

(Beat. Confusion)

SHIRLEY
Yes! To the office!

GAINES
Why would they do that?

FELDSTEIN
To make a point.

SHIRLEY
If the point was to annoy me? It's working.

FELDSTEIN
It's the code.

GAINES
What about it?

STUART
Y'know, Bill, at some point, you're going to have to start paying attention to how this business works.

GAINES
Isn't that why I pay you guys?

(Beat)

STUART
(To FELDSTEIN) How do you argue something like that?

FELDSTEIN
I haven't figured that out yet, either.

SHIRLEY
WHAT DO I DO WITH THESE THINGS!?!

GAINES
Put them in the storeroom.

SHIRLEY
You mean the storeroom where you told me to put the exercise equipment, the ham radio set, the Halloween and Christmas decorations, the Lionel train set, and the eight millimeter home movie set?

GAINES
Right. I guess.

SHIRLEY
It's full.

GAINES
Really?

SHIRLEY
Fine! It's going in here. *(Drops the box)*

GAINES
You can't put it in here!

SHIRLEY
Why not?

GAINES
I work in here!

SHIRLEY
Well, I work out there! *(Turns and starts marching out the door)* Goddamn hoarder. *(Exits)*

FELDSTEIN
We told you moving forward without the code approval was a dicey prospect.

GAINES
They're sending everything back?

(SHIRLEY walks in and drops another box on the floor heavily)

STUART
Looks like it.

(SHIRLEY walks back out)

FELDSTEIN
Doesn't even look like they opened them.

STUART
You figure Goldwater and the others spread the word?

FELDSTEIN
There's plenty of places where newsstands and drug stores are afraid of getting cited...

STUART
Or shut down...

FELDSTEIN
Or worse.

GAINES
But we had the best selling books last year!

(SHIRLEY walks in again and slams down another box. Then she goes back out)

STUART
Bill, you, of all people, know exactly what's going on. Wertham's book, the magazine articles, the book burnings, and then you went on TV and looked like, well...

GAINES
Like what?

(SHIRLEY walks in with another box)

SHIRLEY
You looked like a pervert.

(She slams the box down, as hard as she can)

GAINES
Do you HAVE to do that?

SHIRLEY
I am not going to work in a warehouse!

(She marches out)

STUART
Her description is not inaccurate.

GAINES
She sounds like my father.

(Lights shift, MAX looms)

FELDSTEIN
The distributors won't send them out, the vendors won't put them out, the cops'll cite them for obscenity if they do, or the public will burn them.

(GAINES makes eye contact with the specter of his father)

STUART
What are we going to do, Bill?

(Lights shift, GAINES is caught in a spotlight. MAX continues to loom over him as he speaks)

GAINES
Effectively immediately, EC comics will be ending the runs of our horror and crime comics. I have taken this action based on a premise that has never been proven, that comics are the cause of juvenile delinquency. However, If this is the way the public wants it, it's the way it will have to be, as far as I'm concerned. From now on, all EC Comics publications will be presented with the full approval and seal of the Comics Code Authority, and will include our very exciting new title "Psychoanalysis."

(Projected: The cover of PSYCHOANALYSIS #1)

(MAX hands GAINES a copy of "Tales From the Crypt," which GAINES looks at. MAX smacks GAINES in the shoulder. He holds the comic up and tears it in half. Lights fade out)

SCENE FIVE

(WERTHAM again appears, reading a copy of Psychoanalysis #1)

WERTHAM
It's my premise. I'm a Doctor. He's a failed chemistry teacher with Daddy issues. *(Snaps the comic book closed)* The lesbian counterpart of Batman may be found in the stories of Wonder Woman. For boys, Wonder Woman is a frightening image! The days of sugar, spice and everything nice are long gone.

(Lights shift and WERTHAM fades into the darkness. JANICE and HENRY VALLEAU, her father, enter an office. JANICE is clutching her portfolio)

JANICE
Dad, I don't understand why we stopped here.

HENRY
I just need to make a stop.

JANICE
I'm on deadline, dad! I need to turn these in today. Jobs are scarce now.

HENRY
You need to try something else.

JANICE
We've had this...discussion. I don't want to do anything else.

HENRY
I know. You're an "artist."

JANICE
Yes, I am. A damn good one.

HENRY
Ugh. The language you picked up from those people.

JANICE
You mean my friends?

HENRY
In my experience, friends don't abandon each other.

JANICE
No one abandoned me.

HENRY
That's not what you told your mother.

JANICE
She wasn't supposed to say anything to you...

HENRY
We don't hide things in this family.

JANICE
Well, maybe we'd be better off if we did.

HENRY
What does that mean?

JANICE
It means, this is all none of your business. It means that

the jobs I CAN get right now are few and far between, and I need to get these pages turned in!

HENRY
Keep your voice down.

JANICE
Why? Are these people going to be offended that, for the moment, anyway, I've got a job?

HENRY
Drawing what most people would call filth?

JANICE
Most people don't know what they're talking about. Listening to some wannabe Nazi shrink!

(Lights shift, WERTHAM appears)

WERTHAM
I am NOT, nor have I EVER BEEN, A Nazi.

(Lights shift, WERTHAM disappears)

HENRY
You do not need to yell.

JANICE
What? Are you embarrassed?

HENRY
Yes, you working for those degenerates embarrasses me. That creepy little man on television, those horrible drawings.

JANICE
I have never worked for Gaines, Dad. Frankly, I wasn't good enough. I've never drawn anything that could remotely be called a horror comic.

HENRY
It doesn't matter, you're still tainted.

JANICE
Tainted? Are you going to disown me?

HENRY
No, of course not.

JANICE
Then maybe you should keep your opinion to yourself.

(A well-dressed man, BARRY WALSH, enters)

WALSH
Henry!

HENRY
Barry, how are you?

(They shake)

WALSH
Is this the young lady you've told me so much about?

HENRY
Yes! Barry, this is my daughter, Janice Valleau. Janice, this
is Barry Walsh.

WALSH
Janice. So lovely to meet you, you father has told me so
much about you.

JANICE
Has he?

WALSH
He's told me that you are a very talented young lady.

HENRY
I'm very proud of my little girl.

JANICE
You are?

WALSH
Henry tells me you have a number of skills that we could use here at Walsh, Bullion and Barrett.

JANICE
A job?

HENRY
I have told Barry all about you.

WALSH
It sounds like you'd fit right in.

JANICE
I don't have my full portfolio with me, but I have these pages I was taking over to Charlton...

WALSH
Charlton?

JANICE
Charlton Comics. It's a Nyoka the Jungle Girl strip. It was a bit last-minute, but I made the deadline! I can make deadlines, Mister Walsh. *(She opens her portfolio)* You don't look like a publisher, so I'm guessing advertising. All I have are my narrative strips, but this should give you an idea of my rendering and pencil work.

WALSH
What the devil is this?

HENRY
I'm sorry, Barry.

JANICE
About what?

WALSH
We have an opening in the secretarial pool. Your father

told me that you were looking for work and could type.
I don't know what the heck this is.

HENRY
Barry, she can do the job.

WALSH
It looks like comic books. I don't want anything to do
with that sort of garbage.

JANICE
This is my job.

HENRY
Janice, you need to...

JANICE
I'm an artist.

WALSH
I think the position may be filled.

(JANICE closes her portfolio)

JANICE
That's too bad. My father seemed to really want the job.
He'll be heartbroken!

(JANICE exits, the lights shift)

Scene Six

(WERTHAM steps out of the darkness)

WERTHAM
And so the chickens are coming home to roost, my friends.

(The lights shift to BAKER's apartment. Connie is waiting as BAKER gets dressed to go out)

CONNIE
So I said to her, you better shut your mouth about my boyfriend, because at least he has a damn job!

BAKER
I'm sorry.

CONNIE
She called you a smut peddler. Doesn't that concern you?

BAKER
Not overly.

CONNIE
How can you say that?

BAKER
The ladies down at Miss Ada's Hair Emporium can think whatever they want.

CONNIE
They all have kids, Matt. I'm a little tired of defending you every day at work.

BAKER
Well, tell them to have a bonfire! If it's good enough for Missouri, it's gotta be good enough for New York!

CONNIE
You do not need to yell at me.

(Beat)

BAKER
I'm sorry.

(He takes a couple of deep breaths and rubs his chest)

CONNIE
Are you OK, baby?

BAKER
Hurts.

CONNIE
Did you see the doctor like I told you?

BAKER
Yes! Let it go.

CONNIE
Fine. Have it your way.

(There is a knock at the door, and FRANK GUISTO bursts in waving a newspaper)

GUISTO
Holy shit, Matt!

CONNIE
Goddamn it, Frank!! What have I told you about bursting in here!?

GUISTO
Sorry Connie...Matt, it's Archer.

CONNIE
That publisher friend of yours?

BAKER
What is it?

GUISTO
You need to read it.

(BAKER takes the paper)

BAKER
(Reading) "Archer St John, 54 years old, publisher of Secret Life and other magazines, was found dead yesterday afternoon in the penthouse apartment of a friend, the police reported..."

CONNIE
Was that the guy you worked for?

GUISTO
Can I do anything?

BAKER
Marion McDermott.

CONNIE
Who?

GUISTO
It was her place, Matt.

BAKER
GOD DAMN IDIOT!

(He throws down the paper, and sits, his hand comes to his chest)

CONNIE
Jesus, you seem really upset about some white guy who treated you like the hired help.

GUISTO
Connie, don't...

CONNIE
Oh, put a sock in it, Frank. What the hell is wrong with you, Matt?

BAKER
There is nothing wrong with me.

CONNIE
Why are you acting like this?

BAKER
There was never anything wrong with me.

GUISTO
He never should've...

CONNIE
You two better start making some sort of sense, or I am walking the hell out of here.

BAKER
Why don't you just go, you selfish cow!!

CONNIE
How dare you...

BAKER
Connie, I AM A GAY MAN!

CONNIE
What do you mean?

GUISTO
Calm down, Matt.

BAKER
I like men, Connie. I like to sleep with men! I'm sorry that you were never able to pick up on that, between gossiping at the hair salon and making bitchy comments about the people I work with. Hell, even Frank figured it out on his own.

GUISTO
I did. But, to be fair, I've known him for years.

BAKER
The only man...the only person...I ever came close to truly loving just died.

CONNIE
All this time you let me go on chasing you around, knowing that I was making a fool out of myself!?!

BAKER
I didn't let you do anything. You didn't want to know.

GUISTO
Let's take a breath.

CONNIE
Wertham is right, you're all just a bunch of perverts! *(Grabs her things and heads for the door)* Perverts spreading your filth to children! *(Exits, slamming the door behind her)*

GUISTO
She has a temper, huh?

(BAKER leans on a table clutching his chest, clearly in some distress)

GUISTO
Jesus, Matt. Are you Ok?

BAKER
Where am I supposed to go, Frank?

(GUISTO puts his arms around BAKER, and the lights shift)

SCENE SEVEN

(WERTHAM, once again, steps into the light. He holds the box with the beating heart again)

WERTHAM
Alas, I think it might be broken...

(The heart slows and stops. Lights shift. We find ourselves in JUDGE MURPHY's office at the Comics Code Authority. AL FELDSTEIN sits before him)

FELDSTEIN
Ok, tell me this again...

MURPHY
Mister Feldstein, I see no reason...

FELDSTEIN
We can't have vampires, we can't have werewolves...

MURPHY
Correct.

FELDSTEIN
We can't use zombies...

MURPHY
The walking dead.

FELDSTEIN
That is what I meant.

MURPHY
Are we to revisit the entirety of the code, Mister
Feldstein?

FELDSTEIN
I just don't recall any ban on Martian mutants.

MURPHY
No mutants.

FELDSTEIN
Did you just make that up?

MURPHY
Mutants are verboten.

FELDSTEIN
Is it just that WE, EC comics, have a story that involves
a mutant from Mars?

MURPHY
Mutants are right out.

FELDSTEIN
OK, so what kind of negotiation do we need to have
here?

MURPHY
THE CODE is non-negotiable.

(FELDSTEIN gets up and walks across the stage as the
lights shift into GAINEs' office, where he is waiting
behind his desk)

GAINES
What the hell did he say?

FELDSTEIN
"No mutants."

GAINES
And?

FELDSTEIN
That's it.

GAINES
So what are we supposed to do?

FELDSTEIN
Well, it seems pretty clear he wants us to cut the mutant out of the story.

GAINES
Why?

FELDSTEIN
I don't think I'm qualified to suss out the inner workings of Judge Charles F Murphy.

GAINES
Maybe we should talk to Wertham?

FELDSTEIN
Well, if you want to call him...

(SHIRLEY walks in)

GAINES
Not if you tied a wolverine to my wiener...Oh, jeeze! Sorry Shirley.

SHIRLEY
Wolverine to your wiener...i, e, n, e, r. Do you want me to call someone about that?

GAINES
No.

SHIRLEY
I'm sure I could run down to Times Square and find someone who'll provide that service...

GAINES
Thank you Shirley.

FELDSTEIN
If you have a number, I might take it.

GAINES
And they say I'm a weird guy.

SHIRLEY
You are.

GAINES
Thank you, Shirley.

(He turns back to FELDSTEIN)

GAINES
Can we cut the mutant?

FELDSTEIN
It's the whole story, the mutant's on every page.

SHIRLEY
I wonder if that would be under wolverine or wiener? Oh wait, it's W either way.

GAINES
THANK YOU, SHIRLEY.

SHIRLEY
Do you need anything else?

GAINES
I didn't need anything to begin with! You just came in!

(SHIRLEY starts to exit)

SHIRLEY
Oh, you need plenty. *(Exits)*

GAINES
Why don't I fire her?

FELDSTEIN
What are we going to do? They're clearly going change the rules whenever they want to rein us in.

GAINES
What do we have that we could slot in that they won't shoot down?

FELDSTEIN
We could run Judgment Day again. I don't know what Murphy could object to. It's a preachy, it's anti-racism.

GAINES
You and Joe Orlando's thing? Yeah! There's no way Murphy could have a problem with it.

(FELDSTEIN gets up and walks back to MURPHY's office at the lights shift. He hands the Judgment Day boards to MURPHY)

MURPHY
So let me get this straight. It's a planet of robots?

FELDSTEIN
Exactly.

MURPHY
Living, thinking machines?

FELDSTEIN
Yeah, exactly.

MURPHY
That's an abomination to God, don't you think?

FELDSTEIN
That's not really the point, Judge Murphy.

MURPHY
Oh, I get the point.

FELDSTEIN
I hope so.

MURPHY
What's that!?

FELDSTEIN
Nothing, sir.

MURPHY
Orange robots, and blue robots.

FELDSTEIN
Yes, sir.

MURPHY
And an astronaut comes down to judge them?

FELDSTEIN
Right, Tarlton. Evaluating for entry to the Great Galactic
Republic.

MURPHY
Uh huh.

FELDSTEIN
Make sure they live up to an enlightened standard.

MURPHY
And these blue robots are treated as second class citizens?

FELDSTEIN
Exactly. Inferior housing, working conditions, education.
Segregated restaurants, they're required to sit in the back
of the bus...

(Projected: Panel five of page four of Judgment Day)

(Tarlton: "You differentiate between BLUE robots and ORANGE robots?")

(Orange Robot: "Of course! Otherwise there'd be TROUBLE! Have to keep them in their PLACE, you know!")

FELDSTEIN
Not the most..subtle of allegories, I know, but it is one of our preachies.

MURPHY
Preachies?

FELDSTEIN
Social commentary, American values, that sort of thing.

MURPHY
Good...That's good. So this "Tarlton," he tells these orange robots they have failed, and will be denied entry to this "Great Galactic Republic" thing...

FELDSTEIN
Right, exactly.

MURPHY
Goes back to his ship to fly back to Earth.

FELDSTEIN
Yes, the robot planet has NOT lived up to the values of the Republic, obviously.

MURPHY
He takes off his helmet, and he's black?

(Projected: The final panel of Judgment Day page 7, revealing Tarlton as a Black man)

FELDSTEIN
Ta-dahh!

(Beat)

MURPHY
He can't be Black.

FELDSTEIN
Wait...what?

MURPHY
The book cannot be Code certified if the astronaut, this "Tarlton," is Black.

(MURPHY shoves the boards back at FELDSTEIN. FELDSTEIN gets up, and with a light shift walks back into GAINES' office. STUART is also in the room)

STUART
The guy can't be Black?

FELDSTEIN
That's what the man said.

STUART
Why?

FELDSTEIN
He didn't...really...say....

GAINES
That's the whole Goddamn point!

FELDSTEIN
Well, it appears that's a matter of opinion. As the guy who wrote the thing, I would not say you were incorrect.

STUART
He's just screwing with us.

FELDSTEIN
Y'think?

GAINES
What the hell are we supposed to do?

FELDSTEIN
Just keep going through the files until we find something innocuous enough to appease Murphy?

STUART
What the hell are we going to reprint? If Judgment Day isn't going to pass muster, what do we have that could?

(*GAINES considers for a moment*)

GAINES
Al, get the pages.

STUART
What's the plan?

GAINES
Just get the pages. I'm going over there with you.

(*GAINES marches out into the darkness. FELDSTEIN jumps up to follow*)

FELDSTEIN
You're going?

STUART
Do you really think that's a good idea?!

(*Lights shift as FELDSTEIN crosses back to MURPHY's office. GAINES is already there*)

MURPHY
I think I made our position clear to Mister Feldstein.

GAINES
With all due respect, Mister Murphy...

MURPHY
JUDGE Murphy.

GAINES
Right. How could I forget?

(GAINES reaches out to FELDSTEIN, who hands him the boards)

GAINES
JUDGE Murphy, Judgment Day is one of our most honored and successful stories of social consciousness. Highly respected authors such as Ray Bradbury have sung its praises.

MURPHY
I'm not familiar.

GAINES
You're not familiar with Ray Bradbury?

FELDSTEIN
Well, that explains a hell of a lot.

MURPHY
What was that?

FELDSTEIN
Who, me? Nothing! Nothing at all.

(GAINES displays the boards for MURPHY)

GAINES
The story is an allegory, it's a commentary on the civil rights problems that are, sadly, still percolating in this country. You honestly cannot be blind to this.

MURPHY
Of course not. It's a stain upon our country, as the letter of the code stipulates.

GAINES
The story, Mister Feldstein's writing and Joseph Orlando's art, seeks to expose the youth of America to the failures of our national character that these...crimes of tradition...represent.

MURPHY
Clearly. I am not stupid, Mister Gaines.

GAINES
Then how can you object to the final image? The storytelling choice that clarifies the entire allegory, and brings the indictment of these backward ideas into clear, unambiguous light for the reader!!

(There is a painfully long beat. MURPHY stares at GAINES. The final panel of Judgment Day is once again projected)

MURPHY
The story may run with "Tarlton" as a Black man.

GAINES
Fantastic! I am so glad we were able to come to an agreement!

FELDSTEIN
Thank you, Judge Murphy.

(GAINES and FELDSTEIN begin to gather the boards to leave)

MURPHY
However, you will need to alter the panel to remove the perspiration, the sweat droplets, on this Black man's brow and face.

(GAINES and FELDSTEIN stop cold)

GAINES
I'm sorry. What?

MURPHY
He can't be sweaty.

(The lights shift FELDSTEIN and MURPHY freeze, and MAX GAINES' corpse emerges from the darkness)

MAX
Every day you shame me more. Publishing trash, alienating my friends and colleagues, making a fool out of yourself on national television, tainting my legacy. A spoiled little brat destroying MY company day by day!!!

(The lights shift and Max is gone. The rest of the scene starts again)

MURPHY
Gaines! Did you hear what I said?

FELDSTEIN
Bill?

GAINES
The Black man can't have sweat on his brow?

MURPHY
Absolutely not.

GAINES
Murphy?

MURPHY
That's JUDGE Murphy.

GAINES
FUCK YOU!!

MURPHY
What?

GAINES
I tried to get you all to stand together, and fight back against Wertham and Kefauver. I tried, but you don't give a damn about freedom or art. All you care about is making me, and everyone else, bow down to you! It's not about decency, or justice, or truth...it's about power!

(FELDSTEIN places a hand on GAINES, who shrugs it off)

GAINES
Who cares about government control, government censorship? Not when the artists will gleefully screw each other under the pretense of fear! Do what we tell you to, or we'll shut you down!

(He picks up the Judgment Day boards)

GAINES
This story WILL be published, and maybe every, single issue will come back in unopened boxes! Maybe it'll be the last thing I ever publish, but God damn you and your whole Code, I am going to publish the work I believe in!

MURPHY
Gaines...

GAINES
I've heard all I ever want to from you, JUDGE Murphy. Good day, sir!

(GAINES and FELDSTEIN begin to walk out. The lights start to shift, and WERTHAM begins to move out of the shadows. GAINES stops and stares the old man down)

GAINES
AND I AM FED UP WITH YOU TOO, SAUERKRAUT!!!

(WERTHAM stops cold, and fades back into the shadows. Lights shift)

Scene Eight

(Lights shift to a bar in Manhattan. BAKER and FELDSTEIN are having a drink. Janice sits a few stools away)

BAKER
Did he really say that?

FELDSTEIN
No kidding, Matt. He wanted the sweat removed.

BAKER
Unbelievable.

FELDSTEIN
I'm telling you, I don't know what Gaines is gonna do.

BAKER
He's a weird guy, Al.

FELDSTEIN
I should come down here more often. I miss the shop talk.

(JANICE has noticed their conversation)

JANICE
Bill Gaines? EC Comics? Are you Al Feldstein?

FELDSTEIN
Here it comes...Look, lady...I'm sorry your kid likes our books.

JANICE
I LOVE your books.

(Beat)

FELDSTEIN
Boy, Matt...That's a first.

JANICE
Matt? Matt Baker? You're fantastic! I loved It Rhymes With Lust.

BAKER
You're the one...

JANICE
It was like a bridge between comics and "book" books!

FELDSTEIN
Are we on backwards world?

JANICE
My name is Janice Valleau.

BAKER
Toni Gayle?

FELDSTEIN
And the Betty and Veronica backups for Goldwater?

JANICE
You know my work?

FELDSTEIN
I watch for good artists. It Rhymes With Lust?

BAKER
"Picture novel." Black and white, aimed at a, ah, more
mature audience. Soap opera stuff, really.

FELDSTEIN
Not a comic book?

BAKER
Well, it was, essentially, except for marketing. With the
paperbacks and magazines.

(FELDSTEIN jumps to his feet)

FELDSTEIN
I gotta go! Janice, lovely to meet you. Love your stuff.
Matt? If we have anything....

BAKER
You'll call me, I know.

JANICE
What about me?

FELDSTEIN
On the list! No promises.

(FELDSTEIN rushes out)

BAKER
Never is.

JANICE
What was that?

BAKER
It's EC they're all weird over there.

(Beat)

JANICE
I can't find work.

BAKER
There's been dry spells before.

JANICE
Like this?

BAKER
I don't know.

JANICE
I go to bed every night wondering if those mobs burning books will come for me next. I don't know if I can do it anymore.

BAKER
Sounds like my whole life.

JANICE
I have a young man who wants me to move to Pittsburgh... There's no next job waiting, and I can't stop looking over my shoulder. Sooner or later, I'm going to do something they don't like.

BAKER
Put your heart into your work, and you'll offend somebody.

(BAKER winces, rubs his chest)

JANICE
Are you OK? Do you need...

BAKER
I'm fine, but don't ask my doctor. *(He takes a deep breath)* It figures. The whole business is slipping away, and me with it.

JANICE
All I wanted to do is tell stories. I never thought I'd be terrified to do that.

BAKER
I'm terrified not to.

(Lights shift)

Scene Nine

(Lights up on GAINES' office. GAINES and STUART are sitting around the desk, looking almost shell-shocked. There are liquor bottles and EC comics strewn about, including the latest issue of MAD)

STUART
Can I raise a practical question?

GAINES
Do you have to?

STUART
Somebody probably should.

GAINES
Just have another drink.

STUART
Do I need to fire everyone? Judgment Day will go out in Incredible Science-Fiction number thirty-three, no Code approval...

GAINES
Damn straight.

STUART
...Then what?

(The men fall silent. SHIRLEY enters)

SHIRLEY
Ugh. I should have known. *(Begins to pick up the empties)*
They'll sit here for a month, and the whole office will
smell like a public restroom.

GAINES
Shirley, the company is over. They won.

SHIRLEY
You're just giving up?

(Beat)

GAINES
Yep!

STUART
At least you did get to tell JUDGE Murphy to... *(He
looks to SHIRLEY)*

SHIRLEY
What are you looking at me for? My brothers are
longshoremen.

STUART
You got to tell that jackass to fuck off.

GAINES
Was that worth burning down the whole company?

SHIRLEY
Y'know, this place means a lot to the people who work
here.

STUART
Jeeze, Shirley, I didn't know you cared.

SHIRLEY
Stow it, Lyle, YOU are still a pain in my ass.

GAINES
You don't have to...

SHIRLEY
You made this place your own. Your father, God forgive me, was a bastard. This was grinding sausage to him, and that's all. You gave this place soul.

GAINES
I can't publish comic books without the code, and Murphy clearly isn't going to approve anything worth printing.

(FELDSTEIN bursts into the office)

FELDSTEIN
WHAT IF...we stop publishing comic books?!

STUART
That's pretty much settled, Al.

(FELDSTEIN grabs the copy of MAD)

FELDSTEIN
What about this?

(Projected: The cover of MAD Magazine #30 begins to fade in slowly)

FELDSTEIN
We start publishing it as a full magazine! Just go around the Code all together...

STUART
The Code would still...

FELDSTEIN
No it wouldn't! It only applies to full-color comic books.

Not black and white magazines. Bill, we could publish exactly like we want to, and Goldwater, Murphy, and all the publishers can pound sand!

(GAINES leaps to his feet)

GAINES
Shirley! Get Harvey Kurtzman in here! Al, go out there and get Jack Davis and Will Elder. Lyle, get the printer on the horn and tell them there's going to be a format change!

FELDSTEIN
You got it, boss!

(FELDSTEIN and SHIRLEY hustle out. The MAD cover has fully faded in. STUART starts to head out. GAINES pulls a board of artwork onto his desk, removes his glasses and brings his nose right down to the image, as we saw him in his first meeting with FELDSTEIN. STUART stops short)

STUART
Do you think this is going to work?

(GAINES looks up, and squints at STUART)

GAINES
Y'know, Lyle, all I can say is...What? Me worry?

(Lights smash to black, leaving the MAD cover, which fades. Blackout, Curtain)

END OF PLAY

ABOUT THE PLAYWRIGHT

Mark Pracht was raised in the mountains near Colorado Springs, Colorado. He is Alumni of the University of Nebraska, Kearney, and was a company member of the Sheleterbelt Theatre in Omaha, Nebraska. During that time, he helped develop and produce seven world premiere productions, including his own full-length play, *NEON*.

He's worked as an actor, director and playwright in the Chicago theatre community since 2001, and received the 2019 Joseph Jefferson Award for Best Performance in a Principal Role for his portrayal of Harlan "Mountain" McClintock in Rod Serling's *Requiem for a Heavyweight* at The Artist Home theatre.

His work has been produced in Chicago by Brown Couch Theatre company, where he served as Artistic Director, and Strangeloop theatre.

MORE PLAYS
ON SALE NOW FROM
SORDELET INK
WWW.SORDELETINK.COM

ACTION MOVIE: THE PLAY
JOE FOUST & RICHARD RAGSDALE

You want a play with a car chase, an alligator attack, and a bunch of super-cool fight scenes? Hoo boy, have we got something for you! When wiseacre supervillain John Kreegar gets his filthy mitts on an eldritch artifact of terrible power, everybody's ass is up for grabs! Luckily, the mysterious Dr. Xylene is putting together a fantastic team of good guys to fix Kreegar's wagon but good!

ALL CHILDISH THINGS
JOSEPH ZETTELMAIER

A heist comedy to warm the hearts of Star Wars fans! Dave Bullanski is planning the greatest heist ever. The idea is to take over an old Kenner warehouse and clean out all the rare Star Wars memorabilia, selling it off to a private collector willing to spend $2 million for the loot.

CAMPFIRE
JOSEPH ZETTELMAIER

A horror play. Marcus Carver has brought his niece and nephew back home. In the woods behind his farm, around a campfire, the Carvers will tell stories as they have for many generations. But a stranger has entered the dimly-lit circle.

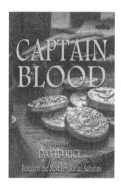

CAPTAIN BLOOD
DAVID RICE

Unjustly sentenced to slavery on a Caribbean island, the bold Dr. Peter Blood falls in love with the lady of the plantation, the lovely Arabella Bishop. When Blood escapes and takes up the life of a pirate, it appears that fate has separated them forever...or has it? Filled with sword fights and pirate battles, love and treachery, and even a song or two, Captain Blood is a pirate adventure perfect for the whole crew!

CHURCHILL
RONALD KEATON

March 1946. After leading Britain and her Allies to victory in the European Theatre, Winston Churchill has been shockingly defeated for re-election as Prime Minister. Living in forced retirement, Churchill receives an invitation from President Harry Truman to speak at Westminster College in Fulton, Missouri, where he will deliver his legendary, emphatic "Iron Curtain" speech.

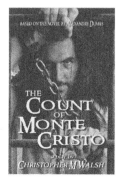

THE COUNT OF MONTE CRISTO
CHRISTOPHER M. WALSH

Framed by a conspiracy and torn from the woman he loves, Edmond Dantes is wrongly imprisoned for fourteen years. Escaping captivity, he enters the upper reaches of Parisian society, insinuating himself into the lives of his three tormentors as, one by one, he seeks to use their own secrets to destroy them in the guise of his new identity: the Count of Monte Cristo. A dark tale of intrigue and vengeance by epic storyteller Alexandre Dumas.

THE DECADE DANCE
JOSEPH ZETTELMAIER

A one-night stand becomes a ten-year journey as Rog and Nina navigate a relationship against the backdrop of a turbulent decade. A touching two-hander, carefully balancing nostalgia, romance, and humor as two people live unexpected lives.

DEAD MAN'S SHOES
Joseph Zettelmaier

A dark and hilarious western, with a dash of buddy-comedy. Notorious outlaw Injun Bill Picote has escaped from prison, along with a hard-luck drunk named Froggy. The unlikely partners endure trials and bizarre misadventures as they set out to right a terrible wrong.

DR. SEWARD'S DRACULA
Joseph Zettelmaier

Dr. Seward has cut himself off from the rest of the world after losing his lover and friends to Dracula. The Irish author Bram Stoker wishes to tell his story. Soon, a series of murders occur, very similar to the ones Seward fought to stop. A re-imagining of Bram Stoker's *Dracula*.

EBENEZER: A Christmas Play
Joseph Zettelmaier

It's a cold Christmas Eve in London, and Ebenezer Scrooge sits in a hospital room. 15 years have passed since his miraculous transformation by the Ghosts of Christmas. They are about to return for a final judgment. Based on Charles Dickens' classic *A Christmas Carol*.

Eve of Ides
David Blixt

The night before his assassination at the hands of conspirators, Julius Caesar attended a feast. With him were Brutus, Cassius, and Antony. During the meal, Caesar was asked what he thought was the best way to die. Caesar answered, 'What does it matter, so long as it's quick?' Based on history and the works of Shakespeare, Eve Of Ides reveals the unexplored relationship between the main players of the age — Caesar, Brutus, and Antony.

FRANKENSTEIN

ROBERT KAUZLARIC

When an unexpected death shatters her family, Victoria retreats into the darkest recesses of her psyche in search of a way forward. To find meaning in this impossible loss, she brings a terrible creation to life — one whose existence threatens all hopes for the future. Haunted and hunted at every turn, Victoria must endure a nightmare journey of the soul in a quest for survival. A brilliant reimagining of the 1818 thriller by Mary Wollstonecraft Shelley.

THE GRAVEDIGGER

JOSEPH ZETTELMAIER

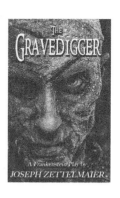

A gothic drama inspired by Mary Shelly's classic novel. In one of Bavaria's forgotten cemeteries, a lone gravedigger discovers a hideously scarred man hiding in a fresh grave. What the gravedigger doesn't know is that the man is none other than the legendary monster created by a mad doctor. What the scarred man doesn't know is the gravedigger's hand in his creation. And what neither men know is that they are hunted by their shared past.

HAUNTED

JOSEPH ZETTELMAIER

"The best way to know a place is through its ghosts." Michigan playwright Joseph Zettelmaier set out to collect a wide variety of ghost stories for this anthology play of true otherworldly encounters by Michiganders from Milan to Marquette.

HAWK'S TAVERN

LORI ROPER & RICK SORDELET

Hawks Tavern centers around estranged African American siblings who reunite amidst catastrophe. Together, they take on revolutionary measures while protecting the family bar amidst the tragic Newark riots of 1967. A bevy of family secrets set the stage for further turmoil in this comic-drama that which insists upon why we can't wait for social justice to heal the wounds suffered by the victimized.

HER MAJESTY'S WILL
ROBERT KAUZLARIC

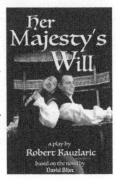

Young William Shakespeare is hiding from the law in rural Lancashire, languishing as a simple school master. Christopher Marlowe is living the high life as a spy for the Crown. When a dastardly plot to assassinate the Queen draws these two unforgettable wits together, Will is swept up in a world of intrigue, treachery, and mayhem in an adventure that will define the rest of his life — if he can only manage to survive it.

IT CAME FROM MARS
JOSEPH ZETTELMAIER

A hilarious look at the night of Orson Welles' famous *War Of The Worlds* broadcast! The members of Farlowe's Mystery Theatre Hour are in rehearsal for their weekly radio show when they hear an alarming announcement come over the radio—Martians have landed! Suddenly secrets are revealed as the cast and crew believe it is their last night on earth!

THE LEAGUE OF AWESOME
CORRBETTE PASKO & SARA SEVIGNY

The superheroes of The League Of Awesome have done it again. They decided to punish the SorrowMaker by trapping him inside a Hardy Boys book. Yeah, it was a little unconventional. Zoe, Sylvia, Penny, Kitty & Rumble wouldn't let him escape. I mean....come on! They'd have to be drunk to do that! Now let's watch them celebrate their victory over him with mojitos. Oh...oh dear.

MALAPERT LOVE
SIAH BERLATSKY

A hilarious mash-up/homage/reimagining of classical comedic elements! *Malapert Love* is a modern response to the tropes, style and structure of Shakespeare's comedies. It follows the tangled and farcical action of a group of people who have all fallen in love with the wrong person.

THE MAN-BEAST
JOSEPH ZETTELMAIER

The wilds of France are stalked by a fearsome creature—the Beast of Gévaudan. An outcast forester presents its corpse to King Louis for a rich reward. However, the story he told may not have been the entire truth. Based on the legends of the loupe-garou, the famous French warewolf.

THE MAN WHO WAS THURSDAY
BILAL DARDAI

When Gabriel Syme joins the undercover detail tasked with infiltrating an anarchists' operations, he soon finds himself sitting on their Supreme Council with the code name "Thursday." It slowly becomes clear that no one in this battle between law and chaos is as they seem — and that Scotland Yard may have created the very problem they're trying to solve. Uncover the truth in this absorbing adaptation of the 1908 satire by G. K. Chesterton.

THE MARK OF KANE
MARK PRACHT

In 1939, two young friends huddled in a Bronx apartment and created a legend, a caped crusader who represents an enduring chapter in the tale of the American comic book. One, Bob Kane, would profit from that legend for years to come. The other, Bill Finger, would be all but forgotten. This is the legacy of the mark of Kane.

THE MOONSTONE
ROBERT KAUZLARIC

The Moonstone, an Indian diamond steeped in a history of violence and mysticism, is stolen from Rachel Verinder's sitting room, and no one in her household is above suspicion. Join an unforgettable collection of liars, lovers, addicts and outcasts as they struggle to uncover the truth and reclaim the stone before its curse destroys them all. This thrilling mystery by Wilkie Collins is regarded as the first detective novel in the English language.

My Italy Story/Long Gone Daddy
Joseph Gallo

Spurred by visits from his grandmother's ghost, Thomas DaGato quits his job as a New York account executive, and travels to the tiny Italian village of his ancestors—Vallata. The sequel play chronicles the comic misadventures of becoming a stay-at-home father.

Once A Ponzi Time
Joe Foust

For years, Harold has 'helped' his friends with their investments, but his artful dodging and shady shenanigans are about to collapse around him as his pyramid scheme tumbles to earth. With only the help of his flakey father, his naive nephew, and a ventriloquist's dummy, can Harold hoodwink the Russian mob, bamboozle the SEC, and restore his friends' fortunes without his entire world becoming a complete farce? Watch him try!

The Scullery Maid
Joseph Zettelmaier

Having declared an uneasy truce in England's ongoing war with France, King Edward III and his nobles celebrate in Nottingham Castle. Unbeknownst to the king, a murder plot is being hatched in the kitchen by the lowliest of his servants, who seeks revenge to right the wrongs of a lifetime. Religion, politics, and questions of loyalty, all at a knife's edge.

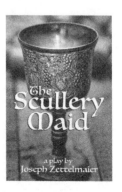

Anton Chekhov's The Seagull
Janice L. Blixt & Alexandra LaCombe

This new translation of Anton Chekhov's classic The Seagull restores what most English-language versions of the play omit: humor. Considered a world-class humorist and wit, Chekov intended this play to be a Comedy. Translated by Alexandra LaCombe and adapted by award-winning director Janice L. Blixt, this is The Seagull audiences have been waiting for.

SEASON ON THE LINE
SHAWN PFAUTSCH

A novice assistant stage manager joins the crew of Bad Settlement Theatre Company for their make-or-break season. An aging artistic director is hell-bent on mounting the elusive perfect staging of Moby Dick. The play swings from soliloquy to action-adventure story as the young man grows to love the theatrical live, even a those around him pay the ultimate price for their pursuit of theatre's own great white whale.

A TALE OF TWO CITIES
CHRISTOPHER M. WALSH

The Reign of Terror sweeps through Paris, and two Londoners are confronted with impossible choices. Will aristocratic Charles Darnay abandon his family to protect an innocent man? Can depressive barrister Sydney Carton make the ultimate sacrifice for unrequited love? An epic story of resurrection and redemption, based on the 1859 novel by Charles Dickens.

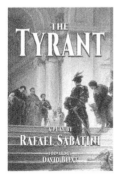

THE TYRANT
RAFAEL SABATINI

Cesare Borgia, former cardinal, Duke of Valentinois and Romanga, tyrant and warlord, has been a figure of awe and scorn for generations. Famed author Rafael Sabatini (*Captain Blood, The Sea Hawk*) returned again and again to this fascinating historical figure's true nature, culminating it a romantic and treacherous piece of theatre.

VOICES IN THE DARK
JOSEPH ZETTELMAIER

Turn out the lights and shiver with delight at this anthology collection of seven short horror radio plays by renowned horror writer Joseph Zettelmaier.

OTHER WORKS FROM
SORDELET INK

WWW.SORDELETINK.COM

HOLD, PLEASE
STAGE MANAGING A PANDEMIC
RICHARD HESTER

A pandemic chronicle from the particular point of view of a career Broadway stage manager living in Manhattan. Part journal, part blog, these essays attempted to make sense of the crisis and what it was doing to us. By the end, everything had changed. What follows is a journey through one of the most fascinating periods in both our cultural and our personal histories.

NELLIE BLY'S WORLD
VOL. 1 - 1887-1888
EDITED BY DAVID BLIXT

Bly's complete reporting, collected for the very first time! Starting with the stunt that made hers a household name, Nellie Bly spends her first year at the New York World going undercover to expose frauds, sharpsters and boodlers, interviewing Belva Lockwood and Hangman Joe, and tackling Phelps the Lobbyist!

NELLIE BLY'S WORLD
VOL. 2 - 1889-1890
EDITED BY DAVID BLIXT

Bly's complete reporting, collected for the very first time! Nellie buys a baby, has herself followed by a detective and arrested, interviews Helen Keller, champion boxer John Sullivan, and convicted would-be killer Eva Hamilton, all before setting out on her greatest stunt of all, a race around the world!

THE MYSTERY OF CENTRAL PARK

A rejected marriage proposal and the corpse of a dead beauty confound Dick Treadwell's hopes for happiness, until his beloved Penelope sets him a task: she will marry him if he solves—*the Mystery of Central Park!*

EVA, THE ADVENTURESS

Nellie Bly's ripped-from-the-headlines novel of a poor girl determined to revenge herself upon the world, only to find that, in the battle between love and revenge, only one can triumph.

NEW YORK BY NIGHT

Setting out to solve the bold diamond robbery, millionaire detective Lionel Dangerfield finds himself in competition with Ruby Sharpe, daring young reporter for the *New York Planet.* Will "The Danger" solve the case before Ruby can steal the story—and his heart?

ALTA LYNN, M.D.

A prank goes awry and Alta Lynn finds herself wed against her will. Leaving love behind, she throws herself into the study of medicine, only to find that love has other plans for her!

WAYNE'S FAITHFUL SWEETHEART

Beautiful Dorette Lover is rescued from poverty when she finds work as an artist's model. That same day she witnesses a seeming murder. To protect the man accused, she agrees to become his bride—only to fall desperately in love with him!

LITTLE LUCKIE

Luckie Thurlow longs to be accepted by society and gain the man she loves. But she harbors a dark secret—she is the daughter of the murderous Gypsy Queen, who plans to use Luckie to gain her own revenge!

IN LOVE WITH A STRANGER

Kit Clarendon is in love! Trouble is, she doesn't know her love's name. But she is determined to track him down and force him to love her! A wild pursuit filled with disguises, desperate deeds, and declarations of love as Kit determines to go through fire and water to win him!

THE LOVE OF THREE GIRLS

An heiress in disguise, a factory girl with dreams of wealth, and a sweet child of charity are forced into rivalry when they all fall in love with the same man! Murder, fever, fallen women, and a desperate villain conspire against—*the love of three girls!*

THE MASTER OF VERONA

Cangrande della Scala is everything a man should be. Daring. Charming. Ruthless. To the poet Dante, he is the ideal Renaissance prince—until Dante's son discovers a secret that could be Cangrande's undoing. Thrust into the betrayal surrounding Verona's prince, Pietro Alighieri must navigate a rivalry that severs a friendship, divides a city, and sparks a feud that will produce Shakespeare's famous star-crossed lovers, Romeo & Juliet.

VOICE OF THE FALCONER

Eight years after the tumultuous events of *The Master of Verona*, Pietro Alaghieri is living in exile in Ravenna, enduring the loss of his famous father while secretly raising Cesco, the bastard heir to Verona's prince, Cangrande della Scala. But young Cesco is determined not to be anyone's pawn. Willful and brilliant, he defies even the stars. Meanwhile, far behind the scenes, a mastermind pulls the strings, moving the players towards a bloody finale.

FORTUNE'S FOOL

While the brilliant, wily young Cesco is schooled in his new duties, Pietro travels to Avignon to fight his excommunication and plead for Cesco's legitimacy, unaware that an old foe has been waiting for this chance to seize control of Verona for himself. Separated from everyone he trusts, Cesco confronts his ambitious cousin, a mysterious murderer, and the Holy Roman Emperor himself. A harrowing series of adventures reveal a secret long hidden, one that threatens Cesco's only chance for true happiness.

THE PRINCE'S DOOM

Heartbroken, Cesco turns his troubled brilliance to darker purposes, embracing a riotous lifestyle in order to challenge the lord of Verona, the Church, and the stars themselves. Trying desperately to salvage what's left of Cesco's spirit, Pietro Alaghieri hopes the intrigues of the Veronese court will shake the young man out of his downward spiral. But when the first body falls, it becomes clear that this new game is deadly, one that will doom them all.

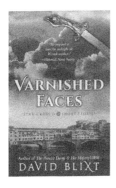

VARNISHED FACES

Collected here are several short stories from the acclaimed Star-Cross'd series, set both within Verona and the world outside its wall. Join Dante's son and Shakespeare's most mercurial creation as they live, love, and lose, seeking their hearts' ease. Filled with swashbuckling adventure, unrequited love, and brutal treachery, this epic journey recalls the best of Bernard Cornwell, Sharon Kay Penman, and Dorothy Dunnett.

HER MAJESTY'S WILL

England, 1586. Swept up in the skirts of a mysterious stranger, Will Shakespeare becomes entangled in a deadly and hilarious misadventure as he accidentally uncovers the Babington Plot: an attempt to murder Queen Elizabeth herself. Aided by the mercurial wit of Kit Marlowe, Will enters London for the first time, chased by rebels, spies, his own government, his past, and a bear. Through it all he demonstrates his loyalty and genius, proving himself to be - Her Majesty's Will.

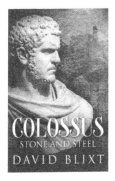

COLOSSUS: STONE & STEEL

Judea, AD 66. A Roman legion suffers a catastrophic defeat at the hands of a band of Hebrews. Knowing Emperor Nero's revenge will be swift, they must decide how to defend their land against the Roman invasion. Caught in the turmoil is Judah: a mason who now finds himself rubbing shoulders with priests, revolutionaries, generals and nobles, drafted to help defend the land of Galilee. Denied the chance to marry, he turns all his energy into defending the besieged city of Jotapata.

COLOSSUS: THE FOUR EMPERORS

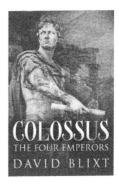

Under Emperor Nero's rule, Rome is a dangerous place. His cruel, artistic whims border on madness, and anyone who dares rise too high has their wings clipped with fatal results. For the Flavius family, this means either promotion or destruction. When Nero is impaled on his own artistry, the whole world is thrown into chaos, and the Flavii must navigate shifting allegiances and murderous alliances as they try to survive the year of the Four Emperors.

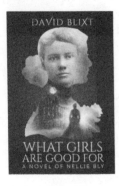

WHAT GIRLS ARE GOOD FOR
A NOVEL OF NELLIE BLY

Nellie Bly has the story of a lifetime. But will she survive to tell it?

Based on the real-life events of the tiny Pennsylvania spitfire who refused to let the world change her, and changed the world instead.

CHARITY GIRL
A NELLIE BLY NOVELETTE

Fresh from her escape from Blackwell's Island, Nellie Bly investigates the doctors who buy and sell babies in Victorian New York. Based on real events and her own reporting, Nellie Bly asks the devastating question - what becomes of babies?

CLEVER GIRL
A NELLIE BLY NOVELLA

A blizzard has frozen all of New York, and Nellie Bly is going stir-crazy when she and Colonel Cockerill plot out her most daring undercover assignment yet: she's going to trap the most crooked man in politics, Edward R. Phelps, the self-styled "King" of the Albany lobby.

FIGHTING WORDS

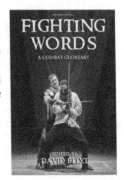

A volume of historical combat terms, as well as essays on broadswords, rapiers, smallswords, and storytelling. Including essays by David Blixt, Jared Kirby, and Mike Leoni, and a glossary of terms culled from The Fightmaster's Companion by Dale Girard.